BACKSEAT FLYERS

Below: F-4Gs (Curtiss Knowles)

BACKSEAT FLYERS

Navigation and Weaponry in the Modern Airplane

Andy Evans

ARMS AND ARMOUR

Arms and Armour Press
A CASSELL IMPRINT
Villiers House, 41-47 Strand, London WC2N 5JE.

Distributed in the USA by Sterling Publishing Co. Inc.,
387 Park Avenue South, New York, NY 10016-8810.

Distributed in Australia by Capricorn Link (Australia)
Pty. Ltd, P.O. Box 665, Lane Cove, New South Wales
2066.

British Library Cataloguing-in-Publication Data: a
catalogue record for this book is available from the
British Library

ISBN 1-85409-153-0

Designed and edited by DAG Publications Ltd.
Designed by David Gibbons; edited by Michael
Boxall; layout by Anthony A. Evans; typeset by Ronset
Typesetters, Darwen, Lancashire; camerawork by M&E
Reproductions, North Fambridge, Essex;
Printed in Singapore by Craft Print Pte, Ltd.

Contents

Introduction	**6**
Ground Attack	**8**
Fleet Defence	**32**
Air Defence	**49**
High-Tech Attackers	**69**
Electronic Warfare &	
Defence Suppression	**88**
Reconnaissance	**102**
Backseat Changes	**124**

Introduction

THE US AIR FORCE call him a 'Wizzo', the US Navy call him a 'RIO', and to the Royal Air Force he's a 'NAV'. Who is he? He belongs to a group of aviators in one of the least explored sectors of airpower today. Often ignored in the face of the more attractive exploits of his partner, he is nevertheless a vital component in today's fast jet aircraft. He is a 'Back Seat Flyer'.

There can be few people who were not impressed by the fictitious performance of 'Maverick' in the hit film *Top Gun*, who it seemed single-handedly dispatched a whole bunch of bad guys, despite the fact that he had a partner in the back seat of his F-14 Tomcat. It appeared that the RIO's contribution to the unfolding events were comparatively small, apart from an attempt at psychology and a few well-chosen superlatives. In the 'real world', however, within the confines of the two-man crew concept, the pilot would have relied heavily on his back-seater to put together the tactical situation and, using the information available to him from all his sensors, provide the pilot with the best opportunity to get in the first shot at any hostiles.

The idea of the two-man crew is not new; its origins can be traced back to the early biplanes and fighters of the First World War. In those days the back-seater held the title of 'Rear-Gunner' or 'Observer', and with the introduction and development of new equipment, he became a 'bomb-aimer and mission specialist'. More and more his role was changing to keep pace with the latest developments. With the introduction of airborne radar and computer-driven avionics, the whole field of the back-seaters' experience changed. He became charged with increasingly sophisticated systems that could not only navigate, but could detect other aircraft and threats, and could deliver weapons precisely on target. His skills were now honed in the understanding of what the array of cockpit sensors were telling him. Working with the pilot to use this information to the best advantage, it becomes a team effort, both parties employed on a successful outcome to the task.

With the technological leaps made in the layout of the fast-jet cockpit, it seems that many aircraft designers still favour the one-man approach. This relies heavily on computerized systems and multi-function displays to present the tactical situations in an understandable manner to the heavily involved one-man operator. High-tech cockpits such as these can be found in the F-16 Fighting Falcon and the F-18 Hornet, both optimized for one-man operation. But there are limits to what a single operator can handle, and despite all the systems in the world, the workload remains high, not to mention that there is still only one pair of the traditional Mk 1 'Eyeballs' available to perform all the tasks required.

With dual-crewed aircraft such as the Tornado, which the RAF operates in both the Ground Attack and Air Defence roles, the pilot and back-seater work together as an integrated unit. Each has his own allotted set of tasks, and this combination gives the aircraft a considerable edge in combat.

Today's fast-jet aircraft are crammed with state of the art avionics, designed to meet and counter any threat to its survival, and it is true that the modern back-seater now spends no more than ten per cent of his time actually doing the traditional job of navigating. Strapped into the back seat, he now takes on the mantle of Mission-Manager, his responsibilities ranging from monitoring the systems to weapons selection, targeting and the effective use of Electronic Countermeasures. In his cockpit he has the very latest in computerized systems, and he must not only know how to operate these, but know how to interpret what they are telling him, and use this information to the best advantage.

Within the pages of this book we will look at the work of several of these hitherto unsung airmen as they do their jobs in a variety of today's high-performance combat aircraft. It must be said that to produce the definitive view on the work of today's back-seater would require more pages than we have available here. However, each chapter will form a small 'vignette' of the differing roles he has in today's airforces, and the aircraft

Below: Fine aerial study of one of the 'Thunder Section' as they formate en route

to meet up with their 'Muds'. (Mark Manwaring)

he flies. We will look at a number of combat types, from the now venerable F-4 Phantom to the ultra high-tech F-15E Strike Eagle, and look at a typical mission through the eyes of the back-seater, ranging from a Combat Air Patrol over

northern England to a high-speed ride on a bombing sortie into Iraq. Each aircraft differs in its systems and its role, but each has one common denominator . . . each carries a 'BACK SEAT FLYER'.

Ground Attack

ONE OF THE FUNDAMENTALS of modern warfare is to deny the enemy the ability to re-supply his front lines by hitting hard at his Command and Control centres, armour and troop concentrations. To that end a number of specialist aircraft have been derived under the general heading of 'Ground Attack'. Despite the workload involved in this most intense aspect of warfare, a large number of these aircraft are single-seaters, but there are a number of dedicated two-seater attack aircraft.

■ **Tornado GR.1.** This is an extremely advanced blind first-pass attack aircraft, designated IDS (Interdictor Strike), with very advanced avionics controlled by the navigator from his rear-seat position. It is able to fly below 200ft at high speed using its excellent Terrain-Following Radar (TFR), and no other aircraft of comparable size is so well equipped to perform the strike task it has been given. In service with the RAF in three variants, the German Air Force, the Italian Air Force and the Royal Saudi Air Force, the Tornado has proven itself to be a very competent aircraft. At the heart of its impressive capabilities is the back-seater's ability to manage the mission, using an array of computerized targeting, navigation and

Below: Tornado GR.1. (Andy Evans)

electronic countermeasures (ECM) systems, that allow the aircraft to carry out its mission at night or in bad weather. A detailed look at the Tornado is found in the Reconnaissance chapter with the GR.1A.

■ **A-6 Intruder.** Designed as a two-seat, carrier-based medium attack aircraft, the A-6 was combat proven in the skies of South East Asia and in the recent Gulf War. Like the USAF's F-111, it employs side-by-side seating, the 'Bombardier-Navigator' occupying the right-hand seat. In the roomy cockpit, which bears more than a passing resemblance to that of the F-111 in its ergonom-

ics, the B/N is able to view nav information, weapons delivery status and basic flight information on a CRT display that allows the A-6 to perform its all-weather/night attack mission. In addition to operating his radar scope, the B/N is also charged with the use of the aircraft's TRAM (Target Recognition and Attack Multisensor). In conjunction with the radar the TRAM aids in target acquisition, the B/N switching to a Forward-looking Infra-red (FLIR) to obtain an enhanced image, mark the designed target with a Laser, and deliver a variety of Smart weapons, in addition to a large number of dumb bombs and TV-guided missiles.

Below: A6E Intruder crew climb aboard. The size of the canopy and apparent width of the cockpit is visible here. (Mike Kopack)

Left: German Tornado IDS. (Stuart Black)

■ **BAe Buccaneer.** On the verge of retirement from the RAF, the Buccaneer has proven itself to be a highly successful low-level strike aircraft, despite very little money having been spent on its avionics systems. Like the Phantom's back-seater, the Buccaneer's Nav has very little room in which to work, but visibility is a little better than in its contemporaries by virtue of a 'stepped' rear cockpit which gives an improved forward view. Originally designed for use by the Royal Navy, it was adopted by the RAF and served for many years in Germany, before being replaced by the Phantom and Jaguar. Currently flying the Maritime Strike role with the RAF, it will soon be replaced by Tornado. In the back seat the Navigator is confronted by very dated technology, using the limited Ferranti Blue Parrot radar which reflected 1950s' thinking! Another duty of the Buccaneer force is that of stand-off designation for laser-guided munitions using the US-designed 'Pave Spike' system, which is controlled by the Nav from a TV tab situated between his legs! During the Gulf War the Buccaneers' back-seaters claimed a little of the limelight with video scenes from their Pave Spike screens giving the TV audiences around the world shots of exploding bridges and the like as they directed laser-guided bombs (LGBs) from RAF Tornados.

Right: Bae Buccaneer in Gulf Colours. (Mark Smith)

Left: US Navy A-6E Intruder. (Curtiss Knowles)

■ **Su-24 Fencer.** The 'Fencer' attack aircraft closely resembles the American F-111, and is one of the Soviet Union's most potent weapons systems. Very little was known about this aircraft and its capabilities until recent times, but with the ending of the Cold War more facts have come to light. The crew accommodation is side-by-side, and access to the wide cockpit is gained through two individual petal-type canopies which, when closed, leave a very restricted view. The pilot occupies the left-hand seat, and the scene in the cockpit is chaotic to say the least. Instruments are entirely conventional, using 1970s' technology,

and both seats have control sticks in front of them. The Navigator, or perhaps Weapons Systems Officer, has a surprising array of equipment at his disposal. The Su-24 is able to deliver a wide variety of ordnance, and the WSO is tasked with the control of the delivery modes, as well as monitoring the RWR, the LO-82 Missile launch locator, radar and Nav systems.

■ **Phantom.** Although dealt with in one of its other guises in another chapter, it is worth noting that the Phantom has served, and continues to serve, with many air arms in the ground-attack

Above: US Navy A-6E Intruder. (Curtiss Knowles)

Opposite page: Two views of the Soviet long range bomber, the Su-24 Fencer: its similarity to the F-111 is clear.

role. Originally designed for carrier operations, it was soon adopted by the US Air Force, where it still serves with a decreasing number of Air National Guard units, as well as with the German, Greek, Turkish, Israeli and Japanese air arms to name but a few. The range of equipment that can be toted by the venerable F-4 is still impressive, and as such the Wizzo in the back seat is a vital member of the team, using his skill to operate the radar, nav systems targeting and weapons delivery. Even though his work area is cramped, he has control of extra equipment added to the cockpit. TV tabs were added to use sensors such as 'Pave Tack' and 'Pave Spike', and the TISEO optical sighting system.

F-111F Liberty Wing Wizzos at War

'The F-111 is basically a 'Wizzo's' airplane,' comments Captain Mark 'Hiebs' Hiebert, an Aardvark right-seater, Senior Captain and Flight Commander with the 'Yellowtails' section of the 493rd Tactical Fighting Wing, flying out of RAF Lakenheath in Suffolk, England. 'The pilot flies the plane, he's the aircraft commander, but to all intents and purposes, he rows the boat and I shoot the ducks. He drives me to work, I deliver the ordnance, kill the target, manage the systems, tell him where to fly and what to do when he gets there, and then he brings me home. He may not agree with that one hundred per cent, but the

Opposite page, top: F-4E Phantom. (Curtiss Knowles)

Opposite page, bottom: Close up as an F-4E tanks. (Curtiss Knowles)

Above: Bae Buccaneer. (Andy Evans)

Below: Carrying two GBU-15 TV-guided bombs, F-111F plugs into a KC-10 Tanker during a training flight, pre-'Desert Storm', over Saudi Arabia. (USAF)

two-man crew concept of the one-eleven is built around the Weapons Systems Officer or WSO (Wizzo) being the mission manager. We also call the pilots WSOs, but to us that stands for Wing Sweep Operator!'

'Hiebs', aged thirty-four, is said by his Squadron Commander, Colonel Mike Malone, to be an 'Old-Timer' on the F-111, having spent just over 900 hours on the type, including 95 combat hours during the Gulf War. He is an ex-'Recce Puke', logging more than 1,050 hours on the RF-4C Phantom before converting to the F-111 in 1986.

Of all the aircraft covered in this book, the F-111 fits less easily into any 'pigeon-hole'. The most obvious difference is that the WSO is not a 'Back Seat Flyer'! In the F-111's cockpit he sits next to the pilot. This type of arrangement is more familiar in training aircraft such as the Jet Provost or the American T-38, but is not seen in any other front-line combat aircraft, with the exception of the Soviet Su-24 Fencer or F-111 ski, which copies the Aardvark's lines quite comprehensively.

'The side-by-side layout has its good points and its bad,' says Hiebs. 'The worst aspect is not being able to "Check your six", unlike in the F-4, which has the traditional tandem seat arrangement, at least then the Wizzo can see behind him! The view back for me in the one-eleven is non-existent and I only really have a fifty per cent ability to check out over the left-hand side. We

Opposite page, top: Captain Mike Russell poses in front of a GBU-15 armed F-111 during 'Desert Storm'. (Captain Mike Russell)

Left: An F-111F carrying two CBU-15 TV guided bombs. (USAF)

Above: Capt Mark Hiebert (right) and Lt Travis Willis discuss and plot the route for a training mission with the 48th TFW. (Andy Evans)

Right: An F-111F formates behind a tanker. (USAF)

have to rely a great deal on crew co-ordination in keeping a sharp look-out.'

As an ex-Phantom flyer, Hiebs concedes his unease at the side-by-side arrangement, having been reared on the WSO being in the 'back seat'. This said, however, the ability for the crew to communicate on a level basis and check each other's moves and cross-monitor systems is a big advantage. 'You have a much more personal flying relationship with the guy in the left-hand seat than if you were just looking at the back of his head!' Hiebs comments.

The F-111 was in many respects a political 'hot-potato', a breakthrough so far as development and technology were concerned, but an operational disappointment in its early deployments in the Vietnam War. However, from the ashes of adversity, it has risen to become one of the most potent weapon platforms of the twentieth century.

In the early 1960s both the US Air Force and the US Navy were looking for a new type of aircraft to see them into the next century. The Air Force was in the market for an aircraft that could carry conventional nuclear weapons over long ranges, flying at tree-top height, and deliver their ordnance with a very high degree of accuracy. This requirement was given the title TFX, or Tactical Fighter Experiment, although how a

'bomber' attracted a 'fighter' prefix is another story. The US Navy was looking for a Fleet Air Defence Fighter or FADF, able to mount long patrols and carry a powerful radar and a heavy load of air-to-air missiles, one of which was the newly developed Hughes AIM 500 Phoenix, destined to be its principal aramament.

The then US Secretary of State, Robert McNamara, having been briefed on both the TFX and FADF projects, and realizing that both programmes would eventually be of great significance, with projected production totals running into the thousands, decided that in order to gain the best value for money the two projects should be amalgamated into one basic airframe design, differing only in its equipment, to fulfil its role within the two services. From this stemmed the drive to reach commonality between the two programmes. The basic design was built around the Air Force's requirements, with little input from the Navy. Curiously it was the Navy who wanted the side-by-side seating and the Air Force who wanted a tandem arrangement! So the F-111A was rolled out to Air Force specifications and the F-111B to the Navy's. After many agonizing problems with the Navy version, in 1968 it was dropped in favour of the Grumman Tomcat.

The Air Force pressed on and eventually produced an aircraft of immense stature that

Left: With a full load of Mk 82 practice bombs, two Liberty Wing F-111s taxi out. (Lieutenant Travis Willis)

Above: The sun glints off the surfaces of the F-111 as it nears its wing man. The Pave Tack pod is stowed in the bulbous fairing just in front of the intakes on the belly, and this will be rolled out when necessary. (Captain Mike Russell)

Below: A dramatic shot of an F-111F blazing off the Lakenheath runway armed with GBU-15 TV-guided bombs. (Andy Evans)

ushered in a new age of military aircraft. With its revolutionary 'swing-wing' design, its ability to make blind first-pass attacks on point targets and its ability to penetrate hostile airspace at low level using its ground-hugging Terrain Following Radar, the F-111 was a force to be reckoned with.

In many ways the F-111 was and is an innovative design, its TFR attack capabilities, unique crew positioning, and fuel capacity for its size being among its very strongest points. 'The F-111 has capabilities that greatly exceed many of the attack airplanes of today,' commented Mark Hiebert. 'Nobody else in the world can do what this airplane does, we have a great TFR, we carry 34,000 pounds of internal gas, we can go twice as far as anybody else and we can designate a target and deliver precision-guided munitions on it. All this flying at 200ft at 600 knots, and come home all survivable. I regard the F-111 as a very, very capable airplane, not as much as my F-4, but there you go!'

What of the aeroplane itself? The 493rd TFW fly the 'F' model, the final tactical version of the Aardvark, some seventy of which were operating out of Lakenheath in early 1992. Featuring all the benefits of the higher-tech avionics of the F-111D, the 'F' Model retains all the capabilities of the 'D', but uses less expensive analogue systems. It also has the most powerful engines of any of the F-111 variants. Its Pratt & Whitney TF30-100s provide 25,100lb of thrust. Couple this with the aircraft's 'Pave Tack' targetting system, allowing the precision delivery of ordnance by day, night or in bad weather, and you can see what makes the F-111F the most potent 'Aardvark' in service.

The 48TFW's first taste of using the F-111F in combat came in the 'El Dorado Canyon' operations, when aircraft were tasked with attacking targets in the Libyan capital of Tripoli in 1986. Because of the capability offered by the Pave Tack system – its accuracy in pin-point attacks, needed to minimize collateral damage – twelve aircraft hit their targets and delivered the required message to the Libyan leader.

In the crews' 'office' the Pilot and WSO are still confronted by traditional 'needle and dial' instruments. The F-111F is a carefully balanced compromise, much better than the 'D' (which incidentally even the most experienced crew cannot fly without an extensive course of instruction) and crossed with the basic 'A' model. The pilot sits on the left-hand side. His front panel is occupied by the flight instruments, to his right is a centre panel between him and the WSO, headed by the

TFR and Radar Homing And Warning Receiver (RHAWR) scopes, and also containing the engine and fuel state gauges. In front of the WSO in the right-hand seat, the instruments are dominated by the attack radar, its scope and panel. Most noticeable is the 'scoop' that covers the radar display and rises out of the panel. This is where the WSO looks 'heads-in' to use the radar, and Pave Tack system. To the left of the 'scoop' are the switches for the Pave Tack system; the WSO develops fingertip control of his sensor equipment when his eyes are buried in his scope. Beneath the scope is his Bomb Navigation Control (BNC) panel, and to its right is the Nuclear Weapons panel which it is to be hoped will never be used. His side consoles contain the radios, IFF and ECM controls, and his so-called (because of its shape!) 'Sheep-Turd' control stick which he uses to steer the radar and Pave Tack systems. Also in the side console is his ordnance set-up panel which he uses to 'cell' his bombs, that is to say set the fuzing and separation parameters.

The WSO also has control of the Nav Attack System (NAS) with a Ballistic Computer Unit (BCU) which 'talks' to the main attack radar to provide an automatic bombing ability if needed. The WSO can also recall any target details entered into the BCU before take-off in order to check that the main radar is on track, and can use this information to allow it to update itself on approach to the target. The WSO controls the jammers and chaff and flare dispensers, and he can see at a glance the number of each type remaining and can select the dispense rate of both items. The pilot's stick is also duplicated in front of the WSO, and he also has the ability to drop any ordnance with his own 'pickle-button'.

So what of the Wizzo himself? Does he have any special attributes? Is he a breed apart? Mark Hiebert continues: 'I don't feel that I possess any special qualities, but to be a flier you do need a certain kind of aptitude, but overall I would say, if I had to pin it down to a few words, then flexibility and diplomacy would fit right in. It helps to be able to work with people especially, being a Wizzo and not the aircraft commander, you have to be a little 'sly' in the way you put ideas into the pilot's head, listen to what he has to say, so you plant the seed of what you think should happen, and make him believe he thought of it first!'

Mark Hiebert has been in the US Air Force for some eleven years, he has been married to Linda, a girl he met while in the service, for seven years, and has been stationed at Lakenheath for the past

Right: A fine study of the Wizzo's position looking back. Captain Mark Hiebert checks his systems. The non-existent rear view is well indicated here. Also of interest is the amount of equipment between the seats. (Captain Mark Hiebert)

Right: Silhouetted against the canopy, Mark Hiebert looks out to check on their wing man. (Captain Mike Russell)

Above left: 'Hiebs', heads in to his radar/Pave Tack scope, uses the side controls to fine tune the image. Note the 'sheep-turd' hand controller by his right hand. (Captain Mike Russell)

Left: Looking over from the pilot's canopy across the Wizzo's position. The Wizzo's bone dome is hung on the 'Scope-Scoop'. Compare

these traditional instruments with the cockpit of the F-15E. (Andy Evans)

Above: After-burners blazing, an F-111F gets airborne from the Lakenheath runway. (Andy Evans)

four years. He was born in Houston, Texas, in 1957 and, his father being in the Air Force, most of his early life was spent in Baltimore, Maryland. 'I joined the Air Force in 1980 and went through a year of undergraduate training, then in the March of eighty-one I was commissioned and went off for pilot training. My goal was to be a Fast Jet jock, and after nine months of training, even though I made the grade, the classes were deemed too large and some people had to go. So the powers that be decided that I should go be a Wizzo. I told them they were communists, but it was either be a Wizzo or be out of the Air Force. I wanted to fly, so I said OK, at least I'll get a fighter, and through that try to get as much 'stick-time' as I can down that route.'

From there 'Hiebs' went to Nav school in 1987, flying in T-43s and T-37s. After learning the basics he went on to Holloman Air Force Base,

flying the T-38 as part of the lead-in fighter training. This is described by Hiebs as a 'Charm-School' for fighter training, learning how to 'Walk'n Talk' fighter language.

'After a spell at survival school to complete my training, in the fall of 1982 I was posted to the RF-4 Phantom at Bergstom Air Force Base in Texas, with the 145th Training Squadron, where I received my MR (Mission Readiness) and subsequently went on to fly the RF-4 for five years. The Phantom was a great aircraft to fly, but I read that the RF-4s were a dying breed, so I took the decision to transition to the F-111, and cross-train while I still had a choice to do so. I figured I could beat the inevitable crowd, and at that point in my career I figured it was a smart thing to do.

'After being accepted for the F-111 I went to Mountain Home Air Force Base to train on the type. I did forty hours in the "A" model, but I

Above: Tanker with 'chicks' in tow. (Mark Hiebert)

wasn't very impressed with the airplane, so when the opportunity arose to either go for the F-111F and be stationed at Upper Heyford or go for the F-111E at Lakenheath, I chose what I considered the better of the two and went for the "F". During my training I saw the Lakenheath guys go to Libya, and I figured if anything was going to happen in the future these guys would be the ones to go out, so for me, this was the place.

'From Phantoms to the F-111A was not very impressive, but when I came to Lakenheath and began flying the F-111F, I was very impressed, and I continue to be pleased with the aircraft's capabilities. I had originally planned to use the F-111F as a stepping-stone to the SR-71, but as that programme has now ended I will probably finish my flying career on the Aardvark.'

The Wizzo's job starts in earnest when he dons his flying-suit and prepares for the mission. Hiebs continues: 'We show up about four hours before take-off at the squadron complex. We check in at the duty desk, which has a large information board behind it. This contains our comprehensive flying schedule, sometimes up to a month in advance. On the board is all the relevant squadron data, such as call-signs, aircraft tail numbers, noted faults and of course which crews are paired up for the day's missions.' For the day's hop

Hiebs will be flying with his Gulf partner, Captain Mark 'Kahuna' Auer. After the check-in, Pilot and Wizzo go into the planning room to look at the day's mission.

'The first thing we check out is the weather,' says Hiebs, 'find out where it's good, and start planning the trip from there. Here in the UK we have set routes to take that avoid restricted areas, and can take us to the ranges or out over the sea. I decide on the target for the day, and get a good ID on the area and work my way back from there. Taking into consideration that the trip will be low and high level, fuel calculations are critical. We take our RTT (Realistic Target Training) very seriously. We look for as realistic or repesentative target as we can, say a factory or an airfield, and plan an attack as if we were really dropping bombs on it. We practise Pave Tack or GBU-15 (TV-guided bombs) precision attacks, that is the way to go in the future, as was proved in the Gulf War. I then do what's called a "six-twentyone", a calculation that gives us a Time-on-Target (TOT), correct fuels and correct headings; this is a manual back-up using the stop-watch and compass methods: Even with all the high-tech systems on board, if we lose one of them we can still count on getting the job done by taking a hack on the watch, a heading and groundspeed.'

Above right: Captain 'Bear' Daughtry reads his flight notes inside the HAS prior to engine start. (Andy Evans)

The crew enter the briefing room where they talk the mission through. The pilot will probably ask the WSO to give him secondary calls on fuel, height, drops and collision avoidance. The Wizzo also sees that the pilot is aware of the ordnance they will be carrying and how it is best delivered. Once they are both happy, it is out to the lockers to suit-up, sign out at the duty desk and step out to the aircraft, about one and a half hours before take-off. Both crew members check the 'externals', usually in the company of the groundcrew chief, and ensure that all panels are closed and the ordnance is correctly loaded. Once satisfied, and while the pilot signs for the aircraft, the Wizzo climbs into the cockpit to start up the systems. The cockpit checks are complex and the aircraft's sophisticated systems take time to warm up and align.

'Once I get in the jet I strap in and get the Inertial Navigation System (INS) set up and give it time to align,' says Hiebs. 'Once that's underway I get the computers up and running and make sure that all the flight information has input to the system. Then I check the Pave Tack pod, and get it boresighted. As the groundcrew instal the pod, I have to ensure that the laser spot is looking in the correct place so that our targetting will be accurate. Then I tune up the radar, check the

ALQ-131 jammer pod, which is installed at the rear of the aircraft, do a chaff and flare check and let the pilot know if we have any snags. With an aircraft with systems such as we have, problems do occur. During this time the pilot has strapped in and wound up the engines and his systems.'

When all systems are functioning correctly, the aircraft is ready to taxi. Call-sign for the mission is 'Deuce 31'. Hiebs checks in with the tower, all is clear, and the aircraft taxis out. 'As we taxi we check the brakes, and check our headings, left and right, and check that the needle and ball indicator is talking to the TFR, and set ourselves up for the last chance End Of the Runway (EOR) checks. Once we are cleared we prepare for take-off. The first thing we do is take out the ejector arming pins. In the F-111 we do not have ejector seats, but the complete cockpit blows out if we have to leave the aeroplane. We then run through our checks.'

HIEBS	AUER
'Rudder Authority Switch'	'Auto'
'Control System Switch'	'Norm'
'Wings, Flaps and Slats'	'16, 25 and Down'
'Fixed Doors Lockout'	'On' (this prevents the wings coming back on take-off)

Left: Ready to roll. (Andy Evans)

Above: Wizzo's instruments and hand controller. (Capt. Mike Russell)

'Ground Air Spoiler and Brake'	'On'
'Speed Brake'	'In'
'Trim'	'Set'
'Check Fuel, should have thirty-two thousand pounds'	'Check'
'Check Feed Tanks'	'Auto'
'Dump'	'Off'
'Tank Feed'	'Auto'
'Check circuit-breakers'	'Check' (these are situated between pilot and WSO and behind the WSO's left shoulder)
'Altitude Cal'	'Check' (checks the system's altitude relative to the ground)
'Buffer Release'	'Check' (this clears out the computer system and initiates the mission status to the crew)

'We then close canopies,' continues Hiebs, 'put our helmet visors down, run through the master caution panel on the pilot's side and acknow-ledge the "contract" that we agreed during the brief. The "contract" is an agreed procedure between me and the pilot, that is purely verbal but it means that we both are aware that if we get a warning or abort at any point during the take-off we both know what procedure to expect.'

'Deuce 31, Ready to roll,' Hiebs announces to the tower. 'Deuce 31 you are cleared for take-off, wind 320 knots at 10".' In the right-hand seat, Mark Hiebert turns on the attack radar and brings the ECM pod to standby, and the lights and beacons come on. Final checks all round, instruments OK, throttles good. Mark Auer pushes them into Full Military Power, the afterburners roar into life, and the aircraft begins to roll.

'During the take-off I am glued to the instruments,' continues Hiebs. 'I am calling out speeds to the pilot and I am focused on the "ERPs" the Engine Pressure Ratios, to ensure we don't lose an engine or a burner, and I keep an eye on all the caution lights.' At 145 knots the pilot unsticks: the take-off has taken a mere fifteen seconds. In full afterburner the aircraft climbs and banks away. Hiebs readies himself for the next phase of the hop.

During the course of a normal training sortie in Europe the F-111 would be heading for the range on bombing practice. How different was the work during January 1991, when the Squadron, including Mark Hiebert and Mark Auer, were based at Taif, Saudi Arabia, at the start of the Gulf War. Nearly all the F-111s of the 493rd TFW were deployed in the war against Iraq, when all the training and experience was put to the test. Let us follow Hiebs as he flies into combat, and see how the mission goes from his position.

'After take-off and we have climbed out on our designated heading, as a Wizzo it's my job now to provide the pacing for the mission. First off I check the weapons panel. On this trip we are carrying four GBU-15 Laser Guided Bombs on the wing pylons, so I set the panel up to give me the fuzing pickle, number and spacing I want for their release. I am also checking the IFF codes, and the TFR, and also I'm navigating along with running through the system, making sure its up to speed. Looking ahead is a big plus, putting into the pilot's head what is due to come next in our sequence. For us right now it's to find our tanker, which should be on the trail ten miles away in our ten o'clock.'

The tanker is met, on time, and the aircraft is topped off with fuel. Once contact is broken the crew set up for the border crossing, current height 17,000ft. 'Just before we cross the border I do a FENCE check, that is to say I run through the Fire control, Emitters, Navigation, Codes and Egress, then as we hit the border the lights go out and I punch up the ECM, put the chaff and flares on line and set up the radar and weapons. Doing this early gives you less to do in the target area, when you will be concentrating on other things. There is an old saying that goes, "The closer you get to a target, the stupider you become", so I try to get my side of things set up well before I get there. I turn up the RHAWR, tweak up the audio so we can hear the threats. Now we are running silent, it's dark outside and the adrenalin is pumping.'

The RHAWR beeps, indicating that systems are looking at them, and they decide it is time to go down to low level. The TFR is set for 500ft, it is engaged and the aircraft points toward the ground; the pilot is now 'hands-off' as the system takes over and levels off at the assigned height. A close look at what's going on around, and the decision to go in at 200ft is taken, so Hiebs steps the TFR down again.

Burning across the desert now at 200ft and 600 knots, the crew speed toward their target, which is Talil airfield, deep in Iraq. The mission calls for them to climb from low level to a higher altitude to deliver their weapons, and as part of a twenty-ship strike package, with support from EF-111's

jammers, F-4G Wild Weasel radar suppression, and F-15 fighter escort, they steel themselves for the task.

Out to the left they start picking up triple-A (anti-aircraft artillery). The RHAWR tells them that it is radar-directed but no threat as the 'Weasels' will soon deal with it. Hiebs checks his systems. The INS tells him that they are fifteen seconds early to their TOT; a quick word with Kahuna and they decide 'to hell with it' press on.

Hiebs looks forward in the plan. In 30 seconds they will reach their first attack Initial Point (IP), which calls for them to climb from 200ft back to 17,000 and begin their bomb run. Passing over a large road, Hiebs again begins to pick up AAA on his side. Momentarily he is distracted by the fireworks, but his training quickly pulls him back to the job in hand. Checking out the INS again shows them slightly left of track, an adjustment to the controls re-aligns the system and the aircraft returns to course. A glance across the instrument panel shows all looks OK. The crew prepare for the climb.

'Confirm switches set up,' calls Hiebs. 'I've got cell one, two, three and six (on the weapons panel) Nav Pickle Button, nose and tail look OK, target ID looks good, twenty seconds to pull-up, TFR good, ECM on line, RHAWR OK, forty miles to target.' Hiebs has a look around, checks over his shoulder and out beyond Mark Auer, a nod says both are in good shape. 'Ten seconds to climb,' calls Hiebs, 'Five . . . four . . . three . . . two . . . one . . . Climb!' Mark Auer pushes up the power, pulls back the stick and the aircraft speeds upwards. 'The first time I did this move I felt totally naked,' continues Mark Hiebert. 'You train to live low down, and now climbing like this, way into bad-guy land, you certainly become more aware of your situation.'

At 17,000 they level off. Again lots of triple-A passes down the left-hand side of the aircraft as they overfly the guns. The shells are fuzing just below the jet, but near enough to illuminate the cockpit interior. 'We hit our second IP again ahead of time, but for now it is not too critical, we are in the "window": As we hit this point I roll down the Pave-Tack pod, ready for the target run.' Hiebs now goes heads-in to his scope, searching the area using the attack radar. 'Minute Forty-Five to pickle,' he reports.

The crew become increasingly aware of the RHAWR panel, situated on the top of the instruments. As it 'beeps and boops' they are aware of the various radars looking at them, to the right, left, in front and behind. Keeping an ear open to

Above: Still from a Pave Tack video, showing Iraqi tank positions as white dots. At the top of the picture and the bottom left the targetting information seen by the Wizzo can be observed. (USAF)

the RHAWR, Hiebs again goes 'heads-in' to his scope for the terminal phase of the run-in. For the duration of this part of the attack the pilot becomes the eyes for both crew, as Hiebs is now totally committed to his work. He is now operating the radar and directing the Pave-Tack system on to his first target. For the Wizzo, this can be an uncomfortable and disorienting time. The Pave-Tack pod has a stabilized image, so no matter what attitude the aircraft takes, the image always stays flat in the scope's screen, and by the nature of the system the Wizzo needs to stay in the scope to ensure that the cross-hairs remain on target. The laser system can automatically track the target, but the Wizzo needs to ensure that this happens, and often needs to make corrections using his hand controller.

The triple-A begins to get intense as they near the target. Mark Auer pulls and weaves the aircraft to avoid the shells, and any possible lock-ups from surface-to-air missiles (SAMs). Mark Hiebert is now concentrating on the ground, and

is being thrown about to some effect! To quote another Wizzo, Lieutenant Travis Willis: 'In a position like this, you're totally heads-in, you're upside down, on your side, pull-G, dump-G, if you puke . . . you go on! A couple of times we dropped our ordnance, and when we rolled out I couldn't tell which way was up for a few moments!'

'System looks good,' says Hiebs. 'Video switch on . . . Sixty seconds to run, confirm "arm" on the pickle button.' He begins slewing the Pave Tack around the target area as the aircraft enters the 'box' at the boundary of their run. Referring to his pre-planned brief, Hiebs locates his first target, and fixes the cross-hairs of the system on a hardened aircraft shelter (HAS).

The Pave-Tack pod has two fields of view, and its Forward Looking Infra-Red sensor provides an x1 or x2 magnified video picture, with a narrow (three degree) or wide (twelve degree) field of view. On to this image is superimposed the laser designator's reticle, as well as a great deal of attack information such as bomb-release parameters and distance and height from the target, and also gives exact angle information for the precision guidance of the bombs.

With the target identified, Hiebs looks to hit his Desired Mean Point of Impact (DMPI, pronounced Dimpey), and with the rest of the formation he has a 'contract' to take out the assigned target. Hiebs tells Kahuna he is 'lasing' on the target and in his scope he can see a flashing white square which shows him where the pod is 'looking'. The return signal from the laser to the pod updates the aircraft's attack systems with accurate information. On his screen Hiebs now sees the laser firing, and the system update, which gives him a time to weapons release and the projected point of impact. 'Clear to drop,' he calls. 'Come around to One-Twenty (degrees).'

The conversation between pilot and Wizzo becomes intense, while they keep an ear cocked to AWACS, the Airborne Warning and Control aircraft which are controlling the overall picture and have spotted possible hostile aircraft threatening the attack formation. Kahuna: 'Thirty Seconds (to release).' Hiebs: 'Scopes are good.' Kahuna: 'Clear to Pickle?' Hiebs: 'Clear.' Kahuna: 'Five seconds . . . four . . . three . . . two . . . one . . . bombs gone!' There is an audible 'thud-thud' as two PGMs (Precision Guided Munitions) fly off the wing pylons. Hiebs: 'Egress heading.' Kahuna: 'OK looking good.' Hiebs: 'Sixty seconds (to impact).'

The aircraft is now banking away from the target and jinking to avoid the defences. The bombs are flying and Hiebs keeps the cross-hairs on track. With the fireworks going on all around them, Mark Auer keeps track of events, while Hiebs is heads-in. Hiebs: 'Come on! . . . come on!' He momentarily loses sight of the target through cloud and smoke. Kahuna: 'Keep on it!' Hiebs: 'Twenty-five seconds (to impact) come left . . . on it . . . fifteen seconds . . . how we doin'?' Kahuna: 'Doin' all right.' Hiebs: 'Five seconds . . . four . . . three . . . two . . . one . . . IMPACT . . . Pow . . . come left One Fifty (degrees).' Kahuna: 'OK' Hiebs: 'Turn . . . Turn . . . looking good.

In his scope Hiebs flicks from the Pave Tack picture to radar. All looks OK, and another flick of the switch returns the Pave Tack to the screen. With the system set on wide, he picks out the next target. Hiebs: 'Pull round, One Six Five degrees, go for next up'. Kahuna: 'Sure, are we havin' fun yet?' Hiebs: 'Thirty seconds to release, I'm on the Dimpey. Scopes good, lasing . . . come left a

little . . . OK!' Kahuna: 'Clear to Pickle?' Hiebs: 'OK!' Down in the scope Hiebs lines up his second target as the aircraft pulls round. The Pave Tack is switched to narrow view and the next aircraft shelter is locked in the cross-hairs. Kahuna: 'Three . . . two . . . one . . . On the Pickle button . . . Bombs-gone . . . bombs gone, chaff-chaff, pick up the egress.' Hiebs: 'Chaff gone.' The aircraft wobbles as the remaining two PGMs leave the pylons. Hiebs: 'Pull One-Two-Eight . . . egress heading One-Eight-Five.' Kahuna: 'OK looking good buddy.' Hiebs: 'Fifty seconds to impact.' Kahuna: 'Rolling out . . . One-Eight-Five . . . looking good.' Hiebs: 'Forty seconds . . . scopes good.' The RHAWR bursts into life with a loud and timely warning . . . Kahuna: 'It's OK, I'm [looking] outside, looking good . . . rolling out, little bit of bank, no lock.' Hiebs: 'Thirty seconds . . . lot of triple A.' Kahuna: 'You're OK.' Hiebs: 'On target, laser locked . . . Twenty-seconds.' Kahuna: 'Doin' real good, little bank . . . scope is good.' Hiebs: 'Fifteen seconds.' Suddenly they get a very strong RHAWR 'BEEP' indicating a lock-up from a radar. Hiebs: 'Check that!' Kahuna: 'I'm outside it's OK, doin' evasive.' Hiebs: 'Ten seconds . . . real good . . . five . . . four . . . three . . . two . . . one . . . IMPACT . . . impact.'

On the Pave Tack screen Hiebs sees his two bombs streak to their target like white bullets, hitting home and blowing dust and debris into the air. Up to this point the crew exchange had been up-beat, reacting to the various threats that were looking at them in a very business-like manner. Without warning the RHAWR bursts out with a signal that freezes the blood of any combat crew.

Kahuna: 'Missile alert! . . . Missile alert!' Hiebs 'Sequence up . . . WHAT?' Kahuna: 'Missile alert!' Hiebs: 'What side?' Kahuna: 'My side left, my side left . . . hang on!' Mark Auer heaves the aircraft into a series of climbing turns, the RHAWR continuing to scream in their ears. Pulling to the left and right the pilot tries to break the lock. Their G-pants grip their legs and abdomen as they pull up. Kahuna: 'Come on! . . . come on!' Hiebs: 'We got it.' The RHAWR stops, the threat is negated, the crew breath a sigh of relief. Hiebs re-assesses the situation, down in the scope he flicks from Pave Tack to radar and back again. Kahuna: 'Coming to One-Nine-Four for the egress . . . rolling out.' Hiebs: 'How we doin?' Kahuna: 'Doin' all right, still a bunch of stuff firing at us.' Hiebs: 'OK on the egress heading . . . let's go home.' Hiebs: 'Scopes good . . . staying on the target for a moment for BDA.'

Right: Looking back on to the pilot's and Wizzo's seats. (Andy Evans)

Kahuna: 'Coming left . . . lots more triple A, we really shook 'em up.' Hiebs: 'Running out go One-Four-Two.'

The targets are blazing wrecks, and the aircraft leave the area. Hiebs gets an update from the radar, and they pull on to a pre-arranged de-confliction heading. As the aircraft makes the turn Hiebs rolls the Pave Tack pod back into the belly of the aircraft. Still flying at 17,000ft, they go back down to low level for the run out to Taif and home. Mark Auer pushes the nose over, sweeps back the wings and the aircraft dives for the ground. Hiebs selects 1,000ft on the TFR. As the aircraft levels out Kahuna kicks in the 'burners for a max-power burst as they leave the area, breaking the sound barrier at low-level. As Hiebs says, 'Hell! I don't care . . . gimme, gimmie gimmie speed!' The night's raid was akin to hitting a home run on a hornets nest with a baseball bat.'

So how has Mark Hieberts career as a Wizzo gone? It has certainly had its moments, as the recounted mission shows. Was it worth all the effort? "On balance I would say my career has gone better than I could have imagined. For a start I was involved in a war that I would never have considered taking place, and I came back in good shape. I had a great time on the F-4, and now some years later I am a Senior Captain, and Flight Commander with the 493rd, and I enjoy immensely all the responsibilities that go with the job. Above all, though, I have had the privilege of flying in the F-111, the primo aircraft for the Wizzo.'

Acknowledgements. Thanks to Captain Mark 'Hiebs' Hiebert and Lieutenant Travis 'Flack' Willis, Wizzos from the 493rd TFW, and to Staff Sergeant Phil Guerrero of the Lakenheath Public Affairs Office.

Fleet Defence

THE US NAVY, possessor of the largest carrier-based air fleet in the world, is the proud owner of arguably the best air-defence aircraft in the shape of the Grumman F-14 Tomcat. Defence of the high-value fleet assets dates back to the Second World War, and generally countries that operate carrier-based aircraft have opted for single-seat fighters, such as the British Sea Harrier, the French Crusader, and soon the French Rafale. The Royal Navy has had a long tradition of using single-seat aircraft, but it has also operated the Phantom and Sea Vixen, both of which have a second crew-member. Currently the US Navy's F-14 stands alone as the only two-seat carrier-based interceptor.

F-14 Tomcat 'Diamondback Rio'

'Diamondback One-Eleven your contact bears zero-three-zero, at ninety miles.' 'Diamondback One-Eleven, Roger, I have the contact; coming to zero-three-zero.' 'Diamondback One-Eleven your contact now bearing zero-five-zero.' 'Diamondback One-Eleven Roger.' 'Bernie come to zero-five-zero, I show contact stacked high and left, come starboard for the hook.'

Does that sound like something from *Top Gun*? Tom Cruise in the front seat? Not exactly, but it is radio contact between an E-2C Hawkeye and the Radar Intercept Officer (RIO) on board an F-14 Tomcat from VF-102 'The Diamondbacks' as they run a practice intercept over the warm waters of the Mediterranean Sea. The RIO in the back seat of the Tomcat is Lieutenant Junior Grade Adrian Marengo-Rowe, call-sign 'Homer'. 'Once we have detected the bad guys, my main job as a RIO is to put us in weapon firing parameters, using the information the radar is giving me. With that I can position the jet in the optimum place for us to launch a "max-range" missile and provide the friendly forces with the longest range protection possible.'

The Grumman F-14 Tomcat is arguably one of the world's greatest interceptors, and it is the lynchpin of the US carrier-borne air-defence. This ultra-capable aircraft carries an unsurpassed array of short- and long-range missiles. At the heart of the Tomcat's performance is the awesome AWG-9 radar and fire-control system coupled to the powerful AIM-54 Phoenix missile which has the capability to track 24 targets and select and attack the six offering the greatest threat. This capacity make the aircraft and its system perhaps the most potent in the skies today. The AIM-54 Phoenix carried by the Tomcat is the longest-range missile ever produced, with an operational range in excess of one hundred nautical miles, and, with its supersonic speed and built-in ECM, it makes for one of the deadliest aircraft/missile combinations ever conceived. In addition to the Phoenix, the Tomcat also carries medium-range radar-guided AIM-7 Sparrow missiles and short-range 'dogfight' AIM-9 Sidewinders, in addition to a 20mm Vulcan cannon.

'For a Naval Flight Officer,' continues Homer, 'the F-14 is the ultimate jet, very powerful and very exciting to fly, and personally I am proud to be part of that combat team. It takes two people to make the Tomcat work; the pilot has his job up front flying the 'plane, and for me in the back seat? Well I guess I am twenty per cent Naval Flight Officer, thirty per cent phychologist and fifty per cent good friend. As far as responsibilities go, well in this airplane mine compare to that of the pilot. I know that in some communities the back-seater is looked on as just that, but not up here.'

'Homer', aged 28, is the son of an RAF Doctor, and was born in Plymouth, England, in 1964. With, a father in the armed forces, he was subject to various postings around the world. The family eventually settled in Dallas, Texas, which is where Homer calls home! So what made Adrian Marengo-Rowe want to become a Naval Aviator?

'When I looked around at the various vocations when I was at high school, it seemed to me that most people in a position of authority or success-ful in their particular field had all had prior military experience,' he says 'So I decided that

Above: The superb visibility for the RIO is amply demonstrated here; he is able to check his deep-six. (Stuart Black)

that was the way to go, so I chose the Navy. There were many reasons behind my decision, there was the travel, the "gloss", the esteem, but mainly it was to get the chance of flying in the ultimate jet . . . the F-14.'

'I originally wanted to be a pilot, but it was clear early on that I was not in possession of the required 20-20 vision, so I was streamed off to become a RIO. I was a college graduate and I received my commission through AOCS, that is the Air Officer Candidate School, whose most famous exploits were shown in the film *An Officer and a Gentleman*, and my basic training was undertaken at NAS Pensacola. The other route into the Navy is through ROTC, the Reserve Office Training Course, which is a college-based programme, unlike AOCS which is a fifteen-week intensive training regime for its candidates. I was at Pensacola for just over a year and that is where I received my most-coveted wings.'

The candidate completes a number of phases on the road to his commission. He begins as an Ensign, and at Pensacola he learns the basics of flight and how to fly. 'The training was intense', continues Homer, 'but I really threw myself into it.' In order to complete their course the embryo

NFOs fly a number of aircraft types. 'I began my flying training on the T-34, which taught me the basics of airmanship. Then I went on to the T-2 Buckeye, where I had my first experience of a carrier landing and a cat-shot. For my role as a NFO I trained in a T-47, which is a militarized Cessna Citation. In this I learned how to use radar systems, how to navigate and how to run intercepts. The T-47 is a pretty benign sort of aircraft. It is not a full flying-suit environment, so when I had completed that phase, it was then on to more fast-jet work in the TA-4J Skyhawk. This aircraft puts you back in full kit, and you re-acquaint yourself with your bone-dome and speed-jeans. Once I had graduated I was posted to Virginia Beach, where I spent about eighteen months of further training, and by this time I had been selected to fly the Tomcat as an RIO, so I had to learn all about her feline ways. At first I thought the training was real difficult, I took it very seriously, and I pushed myself very hard, but once I got into the "click" it started to flow — it was intense, but "doable".

Before we look at the operational role of the Tomcat RIO, what of the aircraft itself? Let us acquaint ourselves with the mighty cat. The F-14 owes its beginnings to a 1960s design, the F-60 Missileer, which was designed to launch the revolutionary Bendix XAA-M10 Eagle missiles at beyond visual range. The Missileer had the capability to guide several missiles to different targets at the same time. Although the project interested the Navy, the Department of Defense had decided on a more 'multi-mission' aircraft, and the programme was cancelled. The Bendix Eagle missile project remained, however, but its future development was transferred to the Hughes Aircraft Corporation, to emerge as the AIM-54 Phoenix.

The search for a common aircraft for both the Air Force and the Navy resulted in the directive that the F-111B, the navalized version, would be tailored to meet the navy's needs. The F-111B proved totally unsuitable for carrier operations and in 1968 the project was cancelled. Grumman had anticipated this collapse and had been privately working on a design of their own. This incorporated the best advantages of the F-111B, such as the Hughes AWG-9 radar system and the Phoenix missiles. This new aircraft design met

with official approval and a contract was awarded. The aircraft included provision not only for the Phoenix, but also for the Sparrow, Sidewinder and cannon armament. Also retained from the One-Eleven were the variable-geometry wings, but the side-by-side seating arrangement was dropped in favour of the traditional tandem arrangement. The new aircraft was designated the F-14 Tomcat, and these new aircraft were first received by VF-124 in 1972. This unit was tasked with training the aircrew for the first two front-line units, VF-1 and VF-2. Currently some 28 squadrons operate the Tomcat, including reserve and training units.

So how does the F-14 RIO do his stuff? Let us go through a carrier launch sequence and a Combat Air Patrol sortie with a Tomcat backseater. Lieutenant Junior Grade Scott 'Raven' Raveling, a recent recruit to the rank of Naval Aviator, is our guide. 'Raven' is 20 years old, has been aboard USS *America* with VF-102 for six months, and is well into his first operational cruise.

The day begins with a detailed brief in VF-102's ready room below decks. This is a comfortable

Below left: 'Raven' deploys the Tomcat's ladder. (Andy Evans)

Right: Diamondback's Tomcat in full burner, gets the 'go' signal before the 'greatest fairground ride in the world'. (US Navy)

Below: F-14 flies close formation. (Stuart Black)

Top left: Wings spread, hook down, nerves jangling, a Tomcat heads for the deck. (Stuart Black)

Left: Tomcat catches the wire, safely aboard. (Stuart Black)

Above: 'Diamondback is in pursuit'. (Stuart Black)

place to be, with several rows of armchair-style seats for the crews and a large video screen at the fore. All the unit's operations are directed from this base.

'Generally I always fly with a senior pilot, although I do train with other front seaters', Raven begins. 'So we are virtually always certain of our crew combination and I am very confident with the abilities of my pilot, who is the most senior in the unit. It's a whole lot better flying with one guy. He knows what to expect from you, and you from him. As the missions go, I could find out as late as 11 o'clock at night just what hop I'll be doing the next day. It may involve low-level or taking pictures of a target, in which case I may have to stay up late and do some planning. I may have to pick out a route, picking up on the IP points, and the like, so that when I arrive at the morning's brief I have all my "preps" in hand.'

'We would normally brief just about two hours before the trip. We all sit in the ready room and watch a TV brief which involves take-off times, when you are going to land, the weather, what frequencies we will be on and what the aims of the hops are. For today it's an AIC scenario, the Diamondbacks will be going to a point out at sea and we will be running intercepts with the other Tomcat unit aboard VF-33, the "Starfighters", and we will be working closely with an EA-6 Prowler Jammer, and an E-2 Hawkeye will be controlling the events. We look at the aircraft involved for the trip, communications, i.e., who we will be talking to, and the Nato code of the day for the IFF authenticator. We also look at "Hot" areas such as restricted airspace, and look at the (Tacan) Tactical Air Navigation frequencies for the trip. This is most important, as most of our fleet ships have a Tacan, so we ensure that that has been thoroughly checked. We will then look at the ordnance we will be carrying, how many of each, and of course all the safety aspects that go with it. Another feature is that of tanking. If we need to use the tanker support, we need to know where he will be.'

'Fuel for us is just too critical. When operating over water we don't want to run out of gas, so one of my main jobs is to monitor the fuel very closely. For today it's ACM (Air Combat Manoeuvring) so we brief our separations in the formation, and what it is going to take to confirm a "kill" during the engagement. For this trip it has been decided that it will be two forward quarter shots, a single bow shot or a roll in from the rear quarter for a kill. We run through our SOPs (Standard Operating Procedures) to ensur that we are all familiar with the "Bible". For example, say something goes wrong and for some reason we get two aircraft converging on each other. The SOP says both aircraft break left to left and these rules don't bend or break, if you want to stay flying or alive.'

Once the crews have gone through this very detailed brief, there remain about 45 minutes to take-off. A short walk down the corridor sees them in the flying-suit room, where they don their kit, collect their 'bone domes' and then go up on deck to the waiting jets. Here they go through a normal 'walk-round' to check for loose or open panels and hydraulic leaks, and inspect the

missiles, to ensure that they all have fins and are correctly mounted. Once the crew are happy they climb aboard. Unlike some modern jets, the Tomcat has its own internal crew access ladder with pull-down steps on the side of the fuselage. 'Raven' climbs into the back seat, straps himself in, connects his G-suit to the aircraft system, and begins to power up the jet.

'I get the ICS and intercom checked, and while I am doing that the pilot gets strapped in and fires up the front seat and winds up the engines. Once he has the engines running he says to me, "OK to start the backseat." "VMC check good," says the pilot. So I start plugging in the circuit-breakers to run the system. I look around the cockpit to ensure that all the switches are set in the correct positions, and then I'm running down the master caution panel, and setting the expendables panel for the chaff and flares. After a couple of minutes the pilot turns on the air-cooling which is my cue to warm up the AWG-9 radar and the INS. The INS aligning process takes about eight to ten minutes, unless we are one of the "Alert" aircraft. Then I can "quick-align" the system, and provided that no-one moves the jet, I have a stored heading alignment which means that we can turn the alert ship in a couple of minutes. During the

Left: Tomcat crew go through checks ready for launch. (Stuart Black)

Above: Ready for the catshot. (Stuart Black)

Right: F-14, wings fully forward, flies into the sunset. (Stuart Black)

start-up sequence the aircraft performs a number of self-tests to determine serviceability, and any problems are flagged up on my TID (Tactical Instrument Display) in the back seat, and I can call a technician to look at the snag.

'Now I am inputting the predetermined way-points into the navigation computer, and then punching in the IFF codes, and then I am set to start the taxi-checks with the pilot. With these completed, which only takes a short while, we check the brakes, and confirm that both front and rear fuel gauges read the same. In all we have fifteen challenge and response checks, and we use a system called "hot-mike" which allows us to talk without pushing buttons. When we are ready we wait for the deck signals officer to tell us that we are expected on the "cat". During this time the pilot fixes his eyes on the deck officer, following his directions implicitly, so now I am watching all around to ensure that we don't hit anything. If I

see anything unsafe I shout "Stop". We wait behind another Tomcat, and as we do the pilot closes the canopy, and we clip on our masks and pull down our visors.

'The catapult officer takes over, as the Tomcat we are behind rides the cat. As we reach the cat-track the pilot "kneels" the aircraft and the deck crew connect us to the shuttle. The pilot spreads the wings, lowers the flaps, checks the spoilers sets the trim and has a look around. The catapult officer cycles the launch, gives us the "T" tension signal with his hands, the pilot runs the engines up to full military power and does a control wipe-out, and I'm looking out around the aircraft to check that all the control surfaces are moving in the correct manner. "Everything looks good," the pilot says. "Yes, looks good back here," I reply. The pilot salutes the cat-officer and pushes the Tomcat into afterburner. The cat-officer kneels, points to the front of the ship and says "see ya",

Above: A view of the RIO's cockpit. (Stuart Black)

Right: 'Raven' deploys the Tomcat's ladder. (Andy Evans)

Right: 'Raven' climbs aboard 'Diamondback 101'. (Andy Evans)

and we are blown off the bow! Zero to 120mph in two seconds, the best fairground ride in the world!'

'During the launch sequence I am constantly monitoring the airspeed and looking for any problems such as a cold cat-shot, a tyre blow or a burner failure, all of which could result in ditching the airplane. We have a "contract" agreed between me and the pilot and this contract is our procedure in the event of a catastrophe. No matter where we are situated, if the aircraft deviates from our agreed parameters, we eject. Our SOPs give me the command ejection sequence, so if I pull the handle, we both go. As an example, if during the cat-shot our airspeed does not reach our limit of 100 knots, no questions, I pull the handle. That's our personal limit, but all RIOs set their own with their pilots. I might see 110 knots during a day launch, and say to the pilot, "Do you have it?", but at night I wouldn't give him that chance!'

'Once we are flying I radio in that we are OK, 'Diamondback One-Eleven airborne'. The pilot retracts the gear, trims the plane, I give him the course and heading and turn on the radar to transmit, check that all my panels are on line, check in with our wingman, and monitor the systems as we transit out to our "Victor-Lima", which is a pre-set point where we will be setting up our CAP to give the Starfighters a run. After about fifteen minutes we reach our patrol spot, and I'm using the radar to scan the area. We get a call from the E-2 Hawkeye that is controlling our intercepts to let us know they have contact with some "trade".'

Raven: 'One-Eleven up for checks.' E-2: 'One-Eleven you are sweet and sweet, cleared to proceed.' Raven: 'One-Eleven Roger, switching to button six. Proceeding to thirty-three Bravo.' E-2: 'One-Eleven you are radar contact, dolly station is in the air.' Raven: 'Roger, One-Eleven is sweet dolly.' Raven confers with his pilot, Commander Luke Parent Call Sign 'Bernie'. Raven: 'Check fuel transfer and pressurization, standby for OBC.' Bernie: 'Good pressure . . . transfer switches are safe.' Raven: 'Good lights . . . OBC checks good . . . my combat checks are com-

Top left: Close formation flying demands 100 per cent concentration. (Stuart Black)

Left: Ready to roll, a Diamondback's Tomcat. (Andy Evans)

plete. Bernie: 'All set up here.' E-2: 'One-Eleven your contacts . . . two up 270 for 60.' Raven: 'One-Eleven. Steady up . . . I show Phoenix selected.' Bernie: 'Concur!' E-2: 'Contacts 265 for 55.' Raven: 'One-Eleven is clean.'

'I update the pilot with positions so that when we hit the point where we can see the bad guys, he knows basically where to expect them to be. I take the heads up from the E-2 and I tune up the radar to acquire the target. I also check with our wingman to ensure that he is looking at the same picture. We have a system in the F-14 called "Flyfire" in which all our aircraft's systems are data-link connected, so that I can see what our wingman sees, and vice-versa.'

'As we break in from the turn I pull a correction to steady our heading . . . "Bernie, come to two-five-zero to stop the drift." E-2: "260 for 50." Raven: "I show a flight of two . . . two mile trail . . . trailers two-thousand feet above . . . stacked right, in combat spread." As we roll in on the attack heading I recall an old saying, that when you go into combat your brain turns to water and pours out of your ears. Raven: "Screwtop, One-Eleven has a single on track, your call angels 20." Raven: "Bernie, check left two-two-zero cut down the aspect, set speed to point nine." Raven: 'Screwtop, confirm weapons status.' E-2: "Simulated Red and free."'

The F-14 prepares for the fray. For Raven the backseat of the Tomcat is an excellent workplace. The ejector seat is cushioned and very comfortable, and the space is impressive for a combat aircraft. In front of him is the circular expanse of the AWG-9 Radar display and his Tactical Display monitors. His position is superb, and with little effort the canopy affords an unsurpassed view all round, especially behind, with the ability to check the 'Deep-Six'. Forward vision is good too, he is able to see over the pilot and through the front windshield, giving him the ability to see the primary flight controls, and more importantly he has a good view of the situation on approach to the carrier. The front seat is optimized for combat, the rear seat is optimized for either long-range tactical work, or shorter-range fighting.

Raven: 'I'm breaking out a second bogey, echelon left . . . trails high . . . come left to centre the "T"'. The 'T' is the radar mark on the AWG-9 that puts the target within the aircraft's system ready to fire the missile. 'The radar can track a multiple of targets in any one of six modes, such as Track While Scan and Pulse Single Target Track. Before we can actually fire a missile the bogey has to be identified hostile with permission to fire. Sometimes we can get a long-range ID from our nose-mounted TCS which is a magnified TV image, or perhaps the Screwtop will already have our permissions ready. We do however have an SOP that allows for redress of any hostile or provoking act, and we are cleared to fire if fired upon. In the Gulf, we set up a "kill-box" over an area, and we knew no friendly forces would be in that vicinity, so anything that flew out of that geographical area that didn't ID up was "dead meat".'

Using every trick available, combat for the RIO is a battle of wits. He has to find the bogey on his scope, and put together the best tactic for the situation. It may be run fast and low, or a dive out of the sun, but whatever it is he has to try to position the jet to avoid contrails, canopy glints, and any untimely radar emissions that could trigger the enemy's Radar Warning Receiver (RWR) to the F-14's presence.

'In the backseat you need your wits about you, you could get so engrossed in flying the perfect intercept that you fail to check your six, and it could get embarrassing if you get bounced by an unseen bogie. Bernie: "T centered." Raven: "Fox three on the leader, fox three on the trailer . . . Bernie Crank right . . . steady up three hundred." Bernie: "Roger . . . Sparrow selected." Raven: "They're fifty left, 35 miles descending through fifteen thousand at one point one . . . right to left pass . . . twenty degrees left aspect . . . center the 'T' for collision." Bernie: "T centered." Raven: "Cut . . . cut . . . GOOD LOCK . . . GOOD LIGHTS . . . FOX THREE ON THE LEADER!"'

Having splashed its first contact, the Tomcat breaks to get a good position and aspect on the second contact. The aircraft is now too close for another Sparrow shot, so the well-proven Sidewinder is brought to bear. Raven: 'Crank right two-eight . . . trailer to the right . . . heading south and high.' Bernie: 'Time out . . . on the leader . . . switching to heat.' Raven: 'Roger . . . come two-fifty.' Bernie: 'I'm tally on the leader . . . on the left of the nose good ID . . . One

Below: The RIO's forward console, dominated by the AWG-9 radar display. Above that is the TID (Tactical Information Display). The amount of space available to the RIO is very evident. (Andy Evans)

Right: Lieutenant Junior Grade Scott 'Raven' Raveling. (Andy Evans)

Below right: The front cockpit of the mighty Tomcat. (Andy Evans)

Starfighter.' The AIM-9 gives the crew the characteristic 'growl' to show that it has acquired the heat source of its intended victim . . . Bernie: 'Good SEAM (Sidewinder Expanded Acquisition Mode) TONE . . . on the trailer.' Raven: 'GOOD TONE . . . FOX 2! . . . Screwtop, Diamondback One-Eleven . . . confirm simulated splash two.' E-2: 'Diamondback One-Eleven . . . confirm.' The exercise complete, Raven and Bernie turn and burn back to the carrier.

The one thing that separates the carrier pilot from others is the carrier landing. Although the crew never give the 'trap' much 'air-time' during the trip, the thought of the return is always in their minds. During the Vietnam War pilots were wired up to check their responses, but the needles on the machines always pegged the highest, not in combat, but when they shot the carrier landings.

The pilot is always being watched and graded on his landing by the Landing Signals Officer (LSO) who is a specially qualified Tomcat pilot, and the last thing he needs while he is under this pressure is any additional hassle from the back seat. 'I always try to be that calm voice behind my pilot,' says Raven. 'Nobody need attitude at this critical time.'

As they approach the ship Raven squares away his systems and prepares to back-up his pilot with information during this crucial phase. 'I sometimes wonder, when I hear of an aircraft that crashes on approach, what the RIO was doing to allow the pilot to fly them into the water. You really have to be sharp. Once we have set ourselves into the landing pattern, we generally settle to the final approach at around three miles aft of the ship and downwind.' Raven: 'Three-

Left: 'Raven' straps into the backseat of his Tomcat and prepares to fire up the systems. Note the level and position of the instruments, relative to his workspace. (Andy Evans)

Right: From behind the cockpit, this shot shows the size of the canopy. (Andy Evans)

hundred knots . . . on approach . . . wings coming forward. . . . Two-fifty . . . wheels coming down . . . all greens. . . . Two-two-five . . . flaps down . . . hook down.' The pilot goes through his final checks, and Raven sets the 'On-Speed' for the landing, depending on fuel and windspeed. Raven: 'Ok . . . on speed One-Four-Two.' Bernie: 'Roger that.'

The pilot now steadies up and looks for the 'Meatball', a series of visually acquired lights which indicate to the pilot his position on the glide path relative to the stern of the ship. LSO: 'Diamondback One-Eleven . . . CALL THE BALL!.' Bernie: 'Roger Ball . . . three-seven [fuel remaining].' For the RIO the final moments are spent calling airspeed and height, backing-up the pilot, and keeping a look-out.

'I'll be updating the pilot as he goes in, like . . .

you're slightly high . . . little left . . and every chance I get I'm checking the ball. We tighten our straps, because when we trap I don't want to eat the radar, and as we approach the fantail I'm listening out to the LSO and watching the airspeed. As we rip over the back of the ship there is a thud as the wheels hit, and the pilot slams the throttles open as we trap a number two wire. BAM! 120 to zero in three seconds . . . we are on the deck. There isn't too much time to think about it, the deck tempo is on-going and the deck-crew are marshalling us into a spot out of the way. I make sure the wings come right back and that again we don't hit anything. Pilots like to catch a number three wire, so I might let him know just that, but if perhaps he only got a two or a one well, I would say, "nope, couldn't see from back here". Diplomacy always!'

'At night the carrier landing is the hardest thing we ever do. Totally different to a day visual trap. It's disorientating, intense and scarey. We set up behind the ship in the same manner as in the day, except I am calling airspeed and height to the pilot ALL the time. He is totally committed to getting us on deck, keeping the wings level, and flying the "ball". As we are established on the pattern, the pilot is checking on his instruments and I'm backing him up with mine. So I would be telling him . . . three miles . . . twelve hundred . . . two-and-a-half . . . one thousand . . . and so on. I do that every quarter of a mile until we are three-quarters of a mile from the ship, when the pilot flies the ball. I also set the ejection system so that I can take us both out, and as we approach I am again keeping an eye on our fuel and height. It's a very strange experience plunging from an ink-black sky on to a carrier: the last seconds you seem to hang in the air until the welcoming thump of the wheels on the deck. My first night trap was a real eye-opener, but I was so glad to be aboard.'

'I suppose I have been lucky so far in that I have flown with a very experienced pilot, and up to now I havn't had a really frightening moment, except one time on finals we flew through a fog bank. I heard the LSO ask the pilot to call the ball. I knew from my instruments we should be in sight of the ship, I was at that moment heads-in and when I heard the pilot say "No I do not have the ball" I said "WHAT!", looked up and all I could see was grey! Thankfully we flew right through it and got down safely. I am proud to be a Naval Flight Officer,' concludes Raven. 'To me it is the most demanding flying job anywhere. In the backseat of the F-14 I am in the ideal aircraft, and I consider I have the finest training in the best service in the world.

As recent history will tell, few who have been foolish enough to pick a fight with a Tomcat have survived to tell the tale, a fitting testament to the thorough professionalism of the Tomcat flyers.

Acknowledgements. Thanks to LTJG Adrian M-Rowe 'Homer' and LTJG Scott Raveling 'Raven' of VF-102 'The Diamondbacks', to Lieutenant Paul Jenkins 'FM Hell' the Public Affairs Officer aboard USS *America*, and to Lieutenant Jack Papp, the US Navy Public Affairs Officer in London.

Above: Approaching the fuel line of a C-130 tanker.

Right: Tornado F.3. (Stuart Black)

Air Defence

ONE OF THE PRIMARY TASKS of any air force is to maintain and defend the integrity of its airspace. From the Spitfires of the Second World War right up to the Tornado ADV of today the fight is the same. Many of today's fast-jet interceptors are single-seaters, which is ideal for point defence or ground-controlled intercepts (GCIs). However, in most cases of aerial combat two heads, or two pairs of eyes, are better than one, as is the case with the Phantom and Tornado.

■ **Tornado F.3 ADV.** In the early 1970s the RAF needed to find a replacement for its Lightning and Phantom interceptors to see it into the next decade. The aircraft had to be capable of mounting long patrols and protecting the UK's large airspace. With the multi-role Tornado IDS (Interdiction Strike) project already under way, a new

variant, the Tornado ADV (Air Defence Variant), specifically designed for the UK's air-defence needs, was proposed. Attaining an 80 per cent commonality with the IDS, the new ADV is able to carry four Sidewinder, four Skyflash and an internal gun, and has a range vastly superior to that of any other RAF fighter. In the backseat the Navigator is confronted by two side-by-side multi-function CRT tabs with two soft key pads by which he can select a number of display modes to manage the Foxhunter radar and the aircraft's weapons systems. Like that of the IDS, the cockpit is comfortable and ergonomically designed, with a high degree of 'user friendliness', that allows the back-seater to carry out his tasks in a good environment, an asset that will stand the RAF in good stead over the years ahead.

■ **MiG-31 Foxhound.** Based on the MiG-25 Foxbat, the MiG-31 is a totally new aircraft. The

major difference is the addition of the second crew member and the vastly improved radar and armament, which include eight AA-9 missiles. The MiG-31 can outrun almost anything else, and has a reported capability to engage multiple targets, obviously putting greater demands on the back-seater.

Phantom FGR2: Tiger Squadron Navigator

'I consider that during my flying career I have been very fortunate. I am currently flying the aircraft I always wanted, on the squadron that I admired, on the station I wanted to be at and doing the job that I set my ambition to do.' So says Flight Lieutenant Mark 'Manners' Manwaring, an RAF fast-jet navigator, flying the McDonnell Douglas Phantom FGR2 with No 74(F) Squadron, the RAF's Tigers, at Wattisham in Suffolk.

'A lot of observers may say that by today's standards the Phantom is outclassed, and a "second-generation" fighter with very dated technology. Bear in mind though, that for all it may lack in current thinking it still carries eight missiles and a massive gun, it has a good radar, and possesses high-speed capabilities at all heights and has the added benefit of two crew

Above: A Tornado F.3 formates with a Canberra. (Stuart Black)

Left: Close up of the cockpit of an F.3. (Andy Evans)

Above right: MiG Foxhound. (Steve Gensler)

Right: Interior of the Tornado F.3 backseat. (BAe)

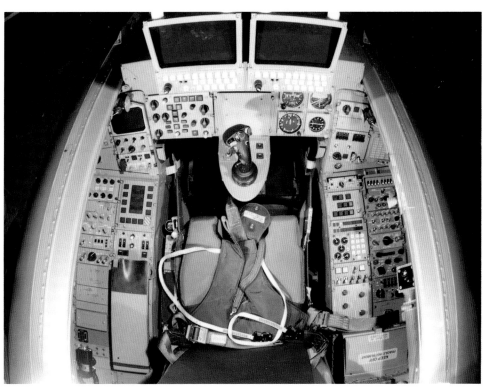

Left: Ground crew aid the pilot and Nav to strap in. (Andy Evans)

Below: Mark Manwaring's Phantom taxies out of its HAS on the Wattisham airfield, and prepares to lead the formation. (Andy Evans)

Below right: Mark Manwaring checks the skies prior to closing the canopies. (Andy Evans)

members. Throughout its service life it has been subject to many systems updates, and what we have now is a much more advanced aircraft than that which entered service in the 1970s. Having said all that, a lot still depends on the abilities of the two people in the aircraft. The Phantom is an intense aircraft to fly as far as workload is concerned, and that is very true of the backseat, and in that environment the crew co-operation is vital to the success of any mission. If we are pitted against a modern agile interceptor the outcome may well benefit the other party, but in situations like that we use every trick in the book to give us a combat edge. Because we are so well-versed in the advantages and limitations of our aircraft we fly more aggressively, more tactically and we fight to win.'

Mark Manwaring, aged 26, is one of the Senior Navigators on the unit, and during his time on the Phantom he has flown with Nos 56 and 74 Squadrons, at RAF Wattisham, and also currently serves on rotation with 1435 Flight at RAF Mount Pleasant in the Falkland Islands. Manners', a native of East Ham in London, joined the Air Force in March 1984, having been in the Air Cadets as a teenager. He has a self-confessed love of aircraft, one of his main reasons for joining the

service. 'While I was in the Cadets I got to see a lot of the Air Force, and the lifestyle as far as I was concerned was fantastic. I was tempted to join the commercial airlines, but that didn't impress me as much as the military, and fast-jet flying is what I wanted to do. My original ideas when I joined the Air Force did not lean toward being a pilot or a navigator, it didn't matter either way, but eventually I chose to be a Nav, as I always said I would rather be a fast-jet navigator than a multi-engined pilot. I can honestly say that I wouldn't swap my position for a job anywhere else in the force, and it will be a sad day when the Phantom retires and Wattisham closes.

'I suppose I have been very lucky. I always wanted to fly the Phantom. I got it, but there were guys on my course at Finningley who didn't get the role they wanted or the particular specialization they were looking for. Me, well I wanted the F-4 from early on, and as my training progressed I took an interest in the aircraft, I found out as much as I could about the F-4, what it did and where it lived, so that when my posting came up I was delighted to get to Wattisham.'

'My initial posting was to No 56 Squadron, and I did a three-year tour with them. I was then lucky enough to get re-posted to No 74 Squadron again

Left: A trio of Phantoms prepare for the break to land. (Andy Evans)

Below left: Dusk shots of Phantom. (Andy Evans)

Below: On rotation to the Falkland Islands, this 1435 Flight aircraft illustrates Mark Manwaring's comment, 'It still carries eight missiles and a massive gun!' (Mark Manwaring)

at Wattisham, at a time when some guys were being streamed on to the Tornado F.3 and others to ground-support jobs. With our commitment in the South Atlantic came the opportunity to serve with 1435 Flight in the Falklands, which certainly makes a change from Europe! Out there the flying is fantastic, and the air combat work is incredible, which rather makes up for the fact that there is absolutely nothing else to do there! Generally I am tasked with a four- to six-weeks rotation, and if required perhaps three times a year.'

So how does 'Manners' regard his role in the back seat of such a 'venerable' aircraft? 'Within the role I find I have all the responsibilities that I expected, and sometimes more than that, but it goes with the territory. There's an awful lot to be aware of flying Air Defence and flying the Phantom. As a senior Nav I find that I fly with a number of less experienced pilots, which makes my job that much harder, as I also adopt the teaching role, but I suppose as the experience increases, so do the responsibilities. Currently my role has expanded to Flight Authorizer, and Air

Combat Leader, things which have widened my horizons in the air.'

To fly the back seat of a Phantom takes a certain kind of airman, as Mark Manwaring describes: 'Capacity is the big thing in the F-4; there is an awful lot of information to disseminate. You also need to have a high standard of mental agility, and even more basic than either of those you need to be numerate – it is a very figure-orientated job. This goes right from the most general briefing slide, to the interpretation of a missile launch parameter, it's all numbers. Many of today's radars display a lot of tactial information to the Nav, such as height, speed, closure rate, etc. In the Phantom most of these scenarios have to be calculated by the Nav or the pilot from the information the system is giving them. So you need to be able to shoulder this additional workload and respond efficiently in a given situation.'

The back seat of the Phantom is, by today's standards, a very cramped place. The view forward is severely restricted by the instrument

panel, with only a small 'tunnel' to the Nav's right-hand side that allows any form of forward vision. Likewise the rear view is virtually non-existent, so the ability to 'Check Six' is virtually nil. Early examples of the British Phantom had glazed centre panels dividing the cockpits, but most of these have now been faired over and the starboard side panel contains a periscopic sighting system with the eyepiece and attendant tubing extending on to the instrument panel. So the back-seater is very much in an enclosed environment, unlike in the F-14 or F-15E discussed in other chapters.

The workload for the navigator is high, and when one confronts the traditional 'needle and dial' instruments, the dated technology becomes apparent. This said, however, the Phantom is still enthused about by its flyers, and remains a potent weapon despite the fact that crews are reliant on very traditional methods of running intercepts. The radar system in the F-4, considered to be the finest in Europe during the 1970s, requires a high degree of 'operator interpretation' from the navigator, and his skills in intercepting targets are tested to the full against more modern fighters such as the F-16 and F-15.

The RAF's involvement with the Phantom is well documented and can be traced back to the mid-sixties, when the Royal Navy ordered an 'Anglicized' version of the US Navy's F-4J, the US-designated F-4K. This aircraft was selected by the Royal Navy in 1964 as a replacement for their subsonic Sea Vixens. The modifications from the basic 'J' to meet British requirements were extensive. The J-79 engines were replaced by Rolls-Royce Speys and this change necessitated enlarging the inlet ducts and engine bays, and the Speys' exhaust nozzles distinguished them from their US counterparts. This new engine was to make the Phantom a faster aircraft, but problems matching it to the airframe led to a loss of performance, and the British version never came up to its 'drawing-board' promise.

Other changes included a fully folding radome, a 40-inch extension to the nosewheel leg and larger flaps and leading edge slats to enable the aircraft to operate from the smaller British carriers, and a navigation suite and cockpits compatible with RAF operating requirements. The first aircraft entered service in 1968, but instead of the expected long-term commitment to the Fleet Air Arm, the Government announced the de-commissioning of the Navy's last carrier, *Ark Royal*, and the transfer of her Phantoms to the RAF.

Above: Tanking from a Tri-Star over the Atlantic. (Mark Manwaring)

Left: Thunder flight taxi to the end of the Wattisham runway. (Mark Manwaring)

Below: Inside the PBF, Mark Manwaring prepares his route plan for the sortie, and prepares one of his briefing slides. (Andy Evans)

Left: Manners straps on his G-Pants. The Phantom crew have to endure the pleasures of an immersion suit worn under their flying gear, which is extremely hot and can get very uncomfortable. (Andy Evans)

Right: Inside the suiting-up room. (Andy Evans)

The RAF had already, independently, placed an order for the Phantom in 1965, after the cancellation of the Hawker P.1154; this was another version based on the F-4J, and was to be designated the F-4M. The Navy's version was called FG.1 by the MOD and the RAF's aircraft was given a more multi-role title of FGR.2. The RAF received its first FGR.2s in 1968, and they began operations with 228 OCU and quickly began to replace the Canberra and Hunter in the strike role. The Phantom was also the possessor of an excellent air-to-air as well as air-to-ground capability, and was seen therefore as a replace-ment for the Lightning in the defence of the UK and Germany. The process of adding the Phan-tom to the air defence arena began with the equipping of No 43 Squadron at Leuchars, in Scotland, with a batch of FG.1s that had been earmarked for the Navy. Hot on their heels was No 111 Squadron, initially equipped with FGR.2s, but re-equipped with the FG.1 on the disbanding of the Navy's only Phantom unit.

Currently the Phantom is in the twilight of its RAF career, only two units remaining, Nos 56 and 74 Squadrons. The other units previously assigned the Phantom have either disbanded or

converted to the more modern Tornado F.3 interceptor. The RAF did however operate a number of Ex-US Navy F-4Js when Britain's air defence commitment was stretched after the recapture of the Falkland Islands and the deployment of an air defence squadron to its protection. The Government purchased fifteen aircraft and issued them to a re-formed 74 Squadron. With increasing numbers of FGR.2s becoming available, as more and more Tornado units formed, they were eventually replaced by the British version in 1991.

As mentioned, the Phantom is still a potent aircraft. Let us look at how the aircraft operates in today's environment as we join Mark Manwaring on a training exercise. 'The sortie will involve a four-ship of Phantoms escorting a formation of Tornado ground-attack aircraft in a simulated strike on Church Fenton airfield in the North of England, and we confidently expect to have a bunch of Tornado F.3s from RAF Leeming on the look-out for us. The mission plan is for us to RV with the Tornados, which will be coming over from Germany, at a point just off Flamborough Head. We will formate and escort them in combat formation across the Teeside Gap, after which the Tornados will break off to attack the airfield, and we will continue to sweep the area around them for hostiles. For this mission we will brief 1½ hours before take-off, and for me, as the formation leader, it is important that all the crews are familiar with the sortie, and up to speed on all our emergency procedures and operating standards. For every sortie there is an Aim, a Scenario and a Threat. Our Aim is Close Escort, the Scenario is Interdiction Support and the Threat is the Defending F.3s. So as I brief the crews, I am trying to be as thorough as I can possibly be.

'For this sortie our call-sign will be "Thunder". Each crew will be assigned an aircraft and told

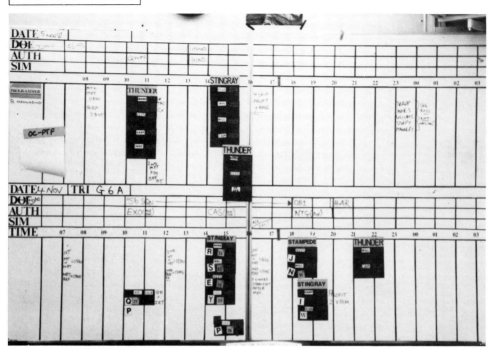

Left: The day's operations are displayed on the board in the PBF. Note the Thunder missions. (Andy Evans)

Left: Mark Manwaring selects one of the systems, pulls on his flying helmet and begins to warm up the rear cockpit. Note the position and size of the circular radar scope in the bottom centre of the panel, and compare that with the Tornado or F-15's displays. Also evident is the near total lack of forward vision. (Andy Evans)

what "fit" it has. All aircraft will have "Charlie" fit, that is two say two wing tanks. It is important that this be noted, as we will all be using fuel at the same rate. If one aircraft had "Bravo" fit, that is one centreline tank, he would be out of the fight twenty minutes early, and I would then need to work out who would break first, and delegate

mission tasks to that crew to suit the need. I look at the Tacan frequency, make sure we all know the setting, and as one of the aircraft in the formation is a 'twin-sticker' without the chaff/flare and sighting facility, I will need to have him in the appropriate slot. Fuel as always is critical, and I need to evaluate sufficient for a diversion – in the event of a problem. "Chicken" is our call-sign for the amount of fuel needed to make the diversion. For this trip it is 35,000 pounds and I also look at our "Bingo" fuel state; if anyone calls "Bingo-One" it means that he has the lowest fuel in the formation and I have to take that problem on board.

'The Met looks OK, our weather diversion is Waddington and our crash diversion is into Coltishall. Finally I look at the emergency of the day. This time it's a birdstrike, so I brief our operating procedure and ensure everyone is current on the SOP. I then look at the chaff and flare settings, and our RWR as we will be going

Left, top and bottom:
The cramped cockpit of the F-4 is well demonstrated here. Note the lack of forward vision and the very closed feeling. (Andy Evans)

against a fighter threat. Call-signs for the other participants will be "Bengal" for the GR.1s and "Scorpion" for the F.3s. Weapons check, pressure settings noted, we will look for an outbrief in about twenty minutes.'

The crews check out at the ops desk and go to the suit-room to collect their flying kit, personal survival suit, g-pants and helmet. The crew 'walk' to the aircraft which are housed inside individual Hardened Aircraft Shelters (HAS) a short distance from the operations centre. As the pilot completes his walk-round checks, Mark Manwaring climbs aboard the Phantom and begins the pre-flight checks. His first job is into the front seat, to check that all there is in order, and ensure that the ground power is feeding into the aircraft. He then climbs into the back seat, checking that his ejection system looks good, and then he proceeds to power up the Intertial Navigation System (INS) to get a good alignment. This takes some time to warm up, but the longer it is left to align the greater its accuracy. Once he has strapped in he does a quick check of his consoles, and settles into his seat. Just above his eyeline is the pin stowage compartment, which he can visually check to see that all the 'pins' that arm his ejector seat are where they should be, commonly called the 'full-five' when all are stowed. Down by his left-hand side he sets his personal weight into the ejector seat's system to adjust the required rocket thrust in case of ejection. He then connects his PEC (Personal Equipment Connector) which gives him oxygen, g-suit inflation and radio communication. With the instrument panel now glowing a dull red, Manners powers up the rest of the systems.

'Initially I check all the circuit-breakers, and check the oxygen, a lamps test and set the cockpit lighting. I select UHF and HF on the radios, and dial in our pre-selected frequencies. Set the Tacan off, punch in the radar camera, do a RWR test, select the upper aerial, check how the INS is looking and set the airfield elevation into the radar altimeter. Adjust the artificial horizon, the air speed Indicator, compass, set 60 chaff and 30 flare and off, and make sure the old 'Nuclear Weapons Consent Switch' is locked off, as I know guys who accidentally "made" this switch and all their tanks punched-off!.' By now the pilot is aboard, and after a check in with him the engines are wound up, and the external power disconnected.

Left: No 74 Squadron's American F-4Js formate en route to their target. (Mark Manwaring)

'I now put the Tacan to standby, radar to B-plus, which energizes the system, check the INS, do a test on the Tacan, and we are set to go. Before we taxi I call the formation on our secure link and ensure that everyone is serviceable, and we taxi out of the HAS after checking in with the tower. I then call the pre-take off checks:

Navigator	Pilot
'Steps'	'Up'
'Oxygen, content-flow and mix'	
'Anti-Icing'	'Normal'
'Bleed Control'	'Normal'
'Trims'	'20 degrees nose down. Aileron and rudder both neutral'
'Attitude Indicator'	'Erect, horizon bars adjusted, the off flag is retracted'
'Compass steering 171'	'171'
'Fuel contents agree'	'Agree'
'Generator warning panel'	'All lights are out'
'Automatic code changer'	'Off'
'Circuit-breakers'	'Good'
'Temperature control'	'Set to Auto'
'Flight Controls . . . check for full and free movement'	'Full and free movement'
'Main brake'	'OK'
'Harnesses (both ensure PEC connected)'	'Check'
'Seats (both check the correct weights are dialled in)'	'Check'
'Seat Pan Handles (both ensure they are free)'	'Check'
'Visors Down'	'Check'
'All Pins stowed'	'Check'

'Manners' checks that the radar display and its hand controller are fully stowed away – the radar scope and controller pull out from the instrument panel and are spring-loaded to snap back into their recess (which sits just in front of the Navigator's knees) if the Nav has to eject. He switches the jettison safety control to ready, and the systems are armed. The canopies are closed and they begin to run through their take-off and emergency checks. As they line up on the runway the last check for 'Manners' is to see that the outer

Above: 'Manners' clips on his mask and continues to fire up the systems in the back seat. The pin stowage and periscopic sighting system are evident. (Andy Evans)

wings are spread and the intake ramps below his cockpit are correctly set.

The pilot pushes the aircraft to full dry power against the brakes, full military power is applied, then into afterburner, the brakes are released and they roar down the Wattisham tarmac. 'As we speed down the runway I am calling out speeds and looking for our specific abort points during the roll. If we have a problem early on we can usually use the brakes and 'chute to stop us in the length of the runway; this is our "V-Stop". Anything above that point we are committed to launch, as we couldn't make the range of the runway. This is our "V-Go". As we reach 135kts we reach that commit point, I call "V-Go" and we unstick. As we are flying into cloud, the other aircraft of the formation use radar to lock on to us as leader, and we do a standard instrument departure at 350kts, trailing each other as we transit the corridor across Coltishall and on to Flamborough Head to meet the Tornados. As we pass over Coltishall we transfer into a "Card Formation" in elements of two aircraft, two miles apart with one mile separation.

'Now as leader I am looking for possible airborne problems, and threats coming in, and weighing up my options, such as peeling off a pair to deal with any incomings. We pick our bombers on time and settle ourselves into form-ation, the Tornados below us. At a point just south of the Amble Light we make a left turn, across Hexam, and past the prominent Bilsdown Mast. Up to this point it has been fairly routine, but I am constantly on the look-out. Just as we cross the Great North Road the RWR lights up in the back, showing that off to the right we are about to be bounced by defending F.3s, possibly a two-ship, with more of their buddies in the area. We always like to Force match, and a check with the other guys confirms that it is a pair of "Scorpions" so I peel off a pair of our Phantoms to deal with them, while we continue on with the Tornado bombers. Within moments the "Muds" turn away to attack Church Fenton, and I begin to pick up a couple of contacts on the radar. We split into a combat pair, mile and a half separa-tion, up now to 450kts, covering each other's six. The radar, in its pulse-doppler mode, picks out two targets heading our way at low level. Using my hand controller I tune in the signal. The radar is looking ten degrees down, we are at 10,000ft, and a quick calculation tells me that the targets are thirty miles away.

'Feeling a bit lucky, I might give them a quick lock with the radar, to get a range, I then work out the closure between us in miles per minute, approximately 15 to 18, and set the stop-watch. I now take Tac-Lead and I inform our number two on the left side . . . "Turning in . . . Turning in Hot".' 'Make a roll out 360 degrees,' Manners tells the pilot. As he rolls out, over the port wing are the two hostiles, Tornado F.3s as expected. 'Got them!' calls 'Manners'. 'Thunder One, 360, two Down.' From that, the Nav in the number two aircraft knows where to look and where to position the jet. The usual practice is to put the threat 'on the nose'. 'I am able, when we lock-up a target, to position a "dot" on the radar display on to the target and from that, again using a calculation, I can work out the hostiles' heading, height and speed.'

'We have a right left crosser, two-one-zero degrees. Heavy crossing, come port forty,' calls Manners. A quick check of the range, and a look at the stopwatch: 25 miles to intercept the target. At twenty miles they begin turning in to attempt to lock-up the Tornados before they can pull out. Spotted, the Tornados turn toward the Phantoms going heavy left, turning in tight to try and get the first shot in. 'Evading Port . . . new heading zero-nine-zero,' announces Manners. 'Hold it there!' A new range now, 18 miles . . . 'Come hard port . . . Steady there!' Manners sees his chance, punches up the numbers on the radar and it locks up. The screen changes to firing mode, and gives him the correct range and velocity to launch a Skyflash missile. On the display, the 'dot' is centered around the target, and this in turn is circled by the 'Available Steering Error Margin', which means that, if the dot remains within the circle, the missile will hit the target. 'Come starboard for the dot,' calls Manners. 'OK . . . come starboard . . . come starboard . . . steady!' 'FOX ONE.'

A press of the trigger and the missile would be away. The Tornado, aware that it has been locked up, desperately tries to evade. Because Skyflash is radar guided, the Phantom must maintain the target within the radar cone. 'Come hard port sixty. Select Sidewinder . . . mash the SEAM (Sidewinder Expanded Acquisition Mode) button.' The heat-seeking Sidewinder is looking in exactly the same place as the radar. In the headset Manners hears the characteristic 'growl' from the missile as it locks-up the target. A quick range check . . . 'Good Lock . . .' 'FOX TWO!'

Simulated 'Winder kill. 'With the Target "splashed" and an F.3 "in the bag", we break radar lock as we blow through. I am also aware of our number two three-quarters of a mile behind

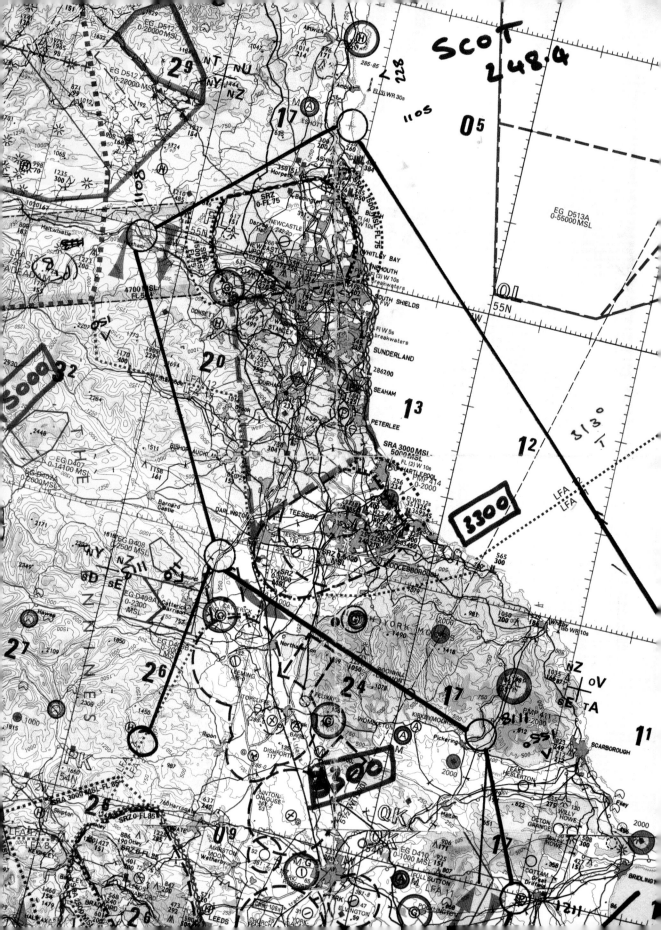

Left: Representative map of the CAP mission described in the text.

Above: Fully armed Phantom ready to go. (Mark Manwaring)

Below: Three greens and everything down as this Firebirds Phantom of No 56 Squadron comes in to land. (Mark Manwaring)

Above: Streaming its brake chute, the Phantom comes to rest. (Andy Evans)

us, also engaged with another F.3. As we continue to scan I pick up another contact, and call "Trailers . . . three-four-zero . . . pair." We turn in for another intercept, but as this pair are much closer in we have to consider actual close fighting. For me in the backseat the job becomes intense, inside and outside the aeroplane. I am trying to keep "tally" on one of the hostiles and trying to find his friend, who has broken off and is waiting for us to get sucked into the fight, so that he can pull behind us for a kill. We will not be that easy to catch. In close combat it is all about angles, especially with the agile modern fighters. This time we got for a minimum separation. I keep a tally on the leader, and the pilot keeps tabs on his No. 2 as we pull round for a max angle turn to try to get an early shot.'

The fight goes on until the purpose of the exercise has been achieved and the 'Knock if off' call is made to all participants. With the fight over the aircraft return to their respective bases, and once down, Mark Manwaring goes through the de-brief and picks up pointers from the sortie, and looks at ways to improve for the next time.

The job of the Phantom navigator is by today's standards a very intense, demanding role, with a lot of reliance placed on the individual skills of the aircrew in obtaining the best from the system. Aircraft like the Tornado F.3 give the back-seater far more information both tactically and navigationally than could ever be expected from the F-4's systems. Mark Manwaring concludes: 'I am proud to fly the Phantom, and to be part of its last days in the RAF. It is still exciting to fly and fight, and I am sure that in many ways nothing will compare to being strapped into its cramped rear cockpit, and blowing-out to take on the "bad guys". It will be a very sad day when I take my final back-seat trip in the trusty Phantom.'

Acknowledgements. Thanks to Flight Lieutenant Mark Manwaring of No 74 Sqn and 1435 Flight, to Mr Michael Hill, CPRO Strike Command, and to Flight Lieutenant David Cutler, the CRO at RAF Wattisham.

High-Tech Attackers

THE PACE at which technology has progressed over the last two decades has led to a new kind of aircraft, and a new breed of high-tech aviators. Cockpits are now filled with computer screens, interfaces, and joysticks, and gone are the traditional displays, although the needle and dial instruments have not been totally abandoned. With this upsurge in new technology, the back-seaters have adapted and risen to the challenge. The USAF upgraded the F-111 with Pave Tack and Pacer Strike, which gave a new lease of life to the Wizzo, but this was merely an update, whereas the latest generation of aircraft are built with the latest technology integral to their success. With the F-15E and the F-18D the Wizzo is a mission specialist, able to use to full effect the computer-driven systems that afford these potent aircraft their amazing capabilities.

■ **Mirage 2000N.** The Mirage 2000 is Dassault's successor to its Mirage III and V aircraft, and represents the ideal application of the tailless delta, making it far superior to any of the previous generations that carry the name 'Mirage'.

Based on the already proven Mirage 2000 two-seat training aircraft, comes the Mirage 2000N. This new variant was born of the French Air Force's need to replace its Mirage III and Jaguar aircraft in the tactical strike role and abandon their free-fall nuclear capability in favour of the Aérospatiale ASMP. Initially given the designation 2000P for 'Pénétration', in order to avoid confusion with any export model, the aircraft was later redesignated 2000N for Nucléaire'. Another new variant was also unveiled in 1989 is the 2000S, for 'Strike', which is an export version of the 2000N, optimized for low-level attack.

In the rear cockpit of these two-seat strikers, the

Below: Mirage 2000N. (Steve Gensler)

Top left: Sand camouflaged Mirage 2000N. (Steve Gensler)

Left: Close up of the Mirage 2000N cockpit, showing to good advantage the rear crew station and its ability to provide the backseater with a reasonable view out. (Steve Gensler)

Above: The US Marines' latest mount, the F-18D Night Attack Hornet. (McDonnell Douglas)

navigator has an impressive array of avionics which enable him to perform the mission tasks. Using the Thomson-CSF-Antelope V radar, with its Terrain Following (TF) and Ground mapping (GM) models, coupled with additional information from the twin SAGEM platforms, the Nav is able to call up a variety of attack and positional information on Thomson-CSF colour CRT displays.

■ **F-18D Night Attack Hornet.** The US Marines have, at the time of writing, begun to make the transition to their latest mount, the F-18D Night Attack Hornet. The addition of an extra crew member has given the Marine aviators a distinct advantage in being able quickly to locate targets, mark them accurately for other forces or themselves, and attack them, delivering precision ordnance by day or night, enhancing their support of the troops on the ground.

Originally intended to replace the Phantom and Skyhawk, the F-18D will also now fill the void created by the cancellation of the A-12 project, and their tasking will include Forward Air Control (FAC), Tactical Recce, and special weapons delivery. The Night Attack Hornet is tailored for two-man operations, using the already proven

two-seat training variant of the Hornet as its basis. The back-seater, known as a Weapons Systems Officer, a term usually associated with the Air Force, has control of the mission from a much improved station. Using the aircraft's Hughes multi-mode radar, night vision goggles (NVGs), the Loral AN/AAs-38 targeting FLIR pod and the Hughes Thermal Imaging Navigation System (TINS), the Night Attack Hornet is a very potent platform.

The aft crew station is 'Mission Configured' for the Wizzo, with the control stick and throttles removed. In front of him are two Multi-Function Displays (MFDs) and a colour Moving Map Display, which are accessed by two systems hand controllers situated on either of the side consoles, one of which also houses his NVGs.

Making their combat debut in 'Desert Storm', the Marines' F-18Ds were given the job of providing 'Fast-FAC', armed with Sidewinder missiles and air-to-ground rockets. Using their night search capabilities to view the target area, the Hornets circled until a contact was made. The 'target' was then marked with white phosphorus rockets, and the WSO used his systems to direct other units into the fray. During the much-publicized Iraqi attack on Khafji, a single F-18D

crew were instrumental in halting an armoured column threatening a Marines outpost.

F-15E Strike Eagle: 'High-Tech Wizzo'

'The F-15E is truly an amazing aircraft. It has superb radar, a highly sophisticated targeting system called Lantirn, and an already well-proven hard-hitting ability by day or night. The jet is fully air-to-air and air-to-ground capable . . . at the same time. This means we can carry a full load of bombs, missiles to protect ourselves, find and designate a target, run our attack at low altitude using the excellent TFR (Terrain Following Radar), and deliver our ordnance with a high degree of accuracy, and quickly egress the area. It's a Wizzo's dream!' These comments on the latest generation of High-Tech-Attack aircraft, the McDonnell Douglas F-15E Strike Eagle, come from Captain Mark 'Bones' Wetzel, a senior Wizzo and a Flight Commander with the 334FW, the 'Fighting Eagles', part of the recently formed 4th Wing at Seymour Johnson Air Force Base in North Carolina.

'For me as a Wizzo, having made the transition from the F-4E Phantom, the new systems and advanced displays and capabilities of the Eagle were a real eye-opener. From the back seat I can manage the whole mission. Just about the only thing I can't do from my position is start the engines! Certainly the plus point of the rear station is that it is definitely "user-friendly", the whole aircraft is tailored to two-man operations, and it utilizes the Wizzo in the back to manage and control the various sensors, and run the task lines of the mission profiles.'

At the heart of the Strike Eagle's impressive capabilities is the Martin-Marietta Lantirn system, an acronym which stands for lo-altitude navigational targeting infra-red for night. This system is considered to be the cream of the current avionics crop, and allows the aircraft to fly at low altitude, under the weather, and mount a precision attack using a variety of guided and unguided ordnance. Lantirn itself consists of two externally mounted pods, located under the engine intakes. The first, the navigation pod, enables the pilot and the Wizzo to 'see in the dark', using an infra-red system that projects a 'night-window' on to the pilot's wide-angle head-up display, and inputs information into the aircraft's flight control systems, enabling it automatically to maintain a pre-

Left: Strike Eagles taxi out for another sortie. (Mike Kopack)

Right: Taking on gas prior to a low-level hop. The shot give a good impression of the size of the cockpit and the space available to the Wizzo in the back seat. (Curtiss Knowles)

selected height in TF mode, totally hands-off. The pod also allows the pilot to 'fly' the aircraft along terrain contours, using the aircraft's high speed and the cover of darkness as it hugs mountains and dives into valleys for cover.

The second pod, the Targeting-Pod, contains a high resolution FLIR, a Laser Designator Rangefinder (for the delivery of PGMs) and a missile boresight correlator for the automatic lock-on of IR Homing Missiles such as the Maverick. Working in conjunction with the Hughes APG-70 Synthetic Aperture Radar, the whole system gives the Echo Eagle an enviable capability. The APG-70 displays a 'bird's-eye-view' of ground targets, projecting a far sharper image of the area as it sweeps. When the desired image of the target area is obtained, the Wizzo can freeze this picture and designate individual targets by posi-

Left, top and bottom: With the LANTIRN system visible under the engine intakes, the Strike Eagle takes on gas. (Curtiss Knowles)

Above: Seymour Johnson-based Strike Eagle. (Mike Kopack)

tioning a cursor over the intended victim. The information is then transferred to the Lantirn system, and the targeting pod locks its tracking FLIR on to the 'dot' which can enable weapons aiming from up to ten miles away. Once locked into the aircraft's system, the automatic tracking system starts and the target information is automatically handed off to the ordnance, which is released at the desired point and guided to the target.

To achieve this high-tech capability, the Wizzo commands an array of equipment which makes his position look more like a computer room than a rear cockpit! Drastically different from the earlier generation two-crew aircraft, the F-15E boasts modern technology which has given it a

very ergonomic appearance. Two six-inch Mono CRT displays are mounted in the centre panel just below eye-level, and these are flanked by two further five-inch colour CRTs, and combined these dominate the forward end of the cockpit.

'One of the main requirements of the Echo-Wizzo,' says Wetzel, 'is "teachability"; you do need a high degree of understanding, not only of the aircraft, but of the sub-systems contained within the computers' menu, and of how to extract and input the information during a busy mission. This said, however, although the systems are computer driven, they are relatively easy to use, and you do need to possess a certain amount of computer literacy and flexibility in your approach. From my point of view the rear

High-Tech Attackers

station is well laid out, and the use of CRTs rather than the traditional needle and dial layout is a real breakthrough. One of the great pluses is that I can set up the displays to "talk to me" in a way that I feel comfortable operating, and I can put menus and systems on to the TV screens in the manner that suits my style of operation by moving them around using my two fixed hand controllers. Unlike the Phantom I used to fly, everything is designed not only to present the "big picture", but also the system status and the tactical situation. As an Ech-Wizzo, my main job is to support the aircraft commander and to get our ordnance on target using all the systems available to me, and ensure we egress safely.'

Mark Wetzel, aged 35, was born in Cincinnatti and currently resides in Corpus Christie, Texas, with his wife and two children. 'I have been in the Air Force for just over ten years, although you may think 35 is a little old for a relatively short career. Well, at the age of 25 I took the decision to make a firm career move and joined the Military. Flying is something I always wanted to do, and having made the decision to join, I wanted to beat the cut-off limit for pilot training. Sadly I didn't make it as a front-seater, but when a

contract was offered to fly the back, I snapped it up. My options, however, were a little limited, either fly a helicopter or fast-jet Wizzo. I went for Wizzo and was accepted and dispatched to Lakeland AFB for officer training in the fall of 1981, and graduated three months later. Scheduled now for Wizzo training, I was sent to Mather in January 1982, and I received my "wings". During that phase I learned my trade in the T-37, doing basics such as DR Nav, low-level point-to-point and running intercepts. I also had my spin training, something I hope never to see again.'

'After a spell at survival school I was sent to "LIFT" (Lead In Fighting Training) at Holloman AFB. Wizzo training took around six weeks, and I was flying in the T-38 and AT-38, and after successful completion I was posted to an RTU (replacement training unit, at Homestead AFB where I was "transitioned" to the F-4D Phantom. From there I joined the 69th TFS, 'the "Dragons", at Moody AFB where I spent just over a year, by now flying the F-4E in the ground-attack mission, not only using conventional bombing skills, but also using Precision Guided Munitions with the Pave Spike designator system. In the fall of 1984 I was posted to Tageu AFB in Korea, where once

Above: At the planning stage of the mission, the pilot, Fred Buttress, discusses the mission plan with Mark Wetzel (left) and his wing man (Steve Henry) on his right. (Andy Evans)

Above left: Bones Wetzel dons his flying gear. (Andy Evans)

Above right: Fully kitted-out, Mark Wetzel checks out his flying-helmet for radio connection and oxygen flow. (Andy Evans)

again I flew the Phantom F-4E, but this time in the Air Defence role. This was a huge challenge as the Korean-based Phantoms were some of the last to fly the air-to-air mode. All told I spent six years there, flying the so-called "Vanilla-E's" without the ARN-101 or the wing-mounted TISEO system.'

'In March 1988 I was re-assigned back to the US, this time to Seymour Johnson AFB with the 334th, but still on the F-4E, returning to the air-to-ground role, specializing in the GBU-15. In 1989 I took the opportunity to transition to the F-15E, as the 334th retired its Phantoms. Because of my previous Wizzo experience I had a shortened

three-month course at Luke AFB to fit me to the F-15E systems.'

The aircraft itself is based on McDonnell Douglas's highly successful F-15B/D airframe, and differs in a number of ways from its air superiority cousins. On the fuselage sides are a pair of conformal fuel tanks, each adding to the aircraft's impressive range. Attached to the CFTs are six tangential weapons pylons, allowing the carriage of stores without the extra drag induced by the traditional MERs. The powerful Vulcan cannon has a new, faster loading system, in addition to the changes in the cockpits.

'As far as the cockpit goes, it's a Wizzo's

47

Left, top and bottom:
Mark Wetzel checks
the Eagle out before
climbing aboard.
(Andy Evans)

delight,' continues Mark Wetzel, 'To be a back-seater in the Strike Eagle is something really special. What is outstanding is the visibility. Compared to a Phantom it is basically unrestricted, 360 degree look-out. There's a lot of room to work, and that allows a feeling of space as well as the view outside. To set up the cockpit for a mission I use two hand controllers, one on each of the side consoles, to select the menus on the CRTs. The displays are backed-up with some instruments at knee level, and on the side consoles are the switches that run the Lantirn system, radios, ECM, chaff and flares and emergency canopy releases. Down by my right knee is the "Up Front Controller" (UFC) which is set at an angle that facilitates easier punching of its keys. This is the main bridge between man and

machine, and is the central interface with the main computer. The CRTs are pretty neat, and present the information in a very clear manner. The information can be input to the computer by using the UFC or a Data Transfer Module, the DTM (similar in operation to that used by the RAF's Jaguars, where the information is input at a ground station and stored in an electronic block for later transfer to the aircraft's system). The CRT displays have twenty buttons around them and I use these to extract the specific data I need, dependent on the screen I am accessing. As mentioned, the rear cockpit is individually programmable and the way I set up the back-seat may be totally different from the next back-seater who uses the jet.

'One of the main inputs to the system is to tell it

Right: Up the ladder
into the backseat.
(Andy Evans)

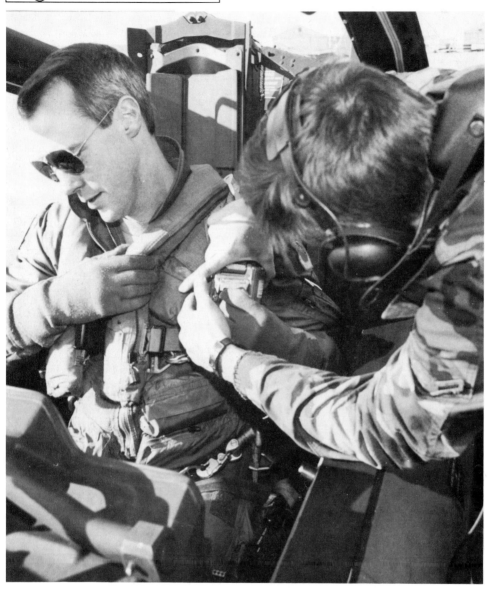

Left: Ground crew help 'Bones' to strap in to the roomy back seat, and he dons his flying-helmet and prepares to fire up the systems. (Andy Evans)

Right, top and bottom: 'At the heart of the Strike Eagle's impressive capabilities is the Martin Lantirn System'. Seen here is the Targetting pod and Navigation pod fitted under the engine intakes. (Andy Evans)

what weapons we are carrying. Sometimes this is done on the DTM, but I like to set the number and separation and whether it will be a manual or automatic release. I also like to set the fuzing – essential, this, for a low-altitude attack. This section of the system is called the PAC (Programmable Armament Computer). One of the other nice things is a full set of flight controls, the full nine yards, as we say.'

Having looked at the man and the machine, let us follow Mark Wetzel as he prepares for a combat hop, and learn how his training set him in good stead on the first night of the Gulf War. 'We normally brief two hours before the trip. This takes around an hour and a quarter to complete, and before this we would have planned the trip well in advance, gathering target information, threats, weather and fuel needed, and logging all the essential flight data into the DTM. One of the joys of the F-15E is the excellent moving-map display which obviates the need for the Wizzo to take a huge "leg-full" of maps with him! Walk-round takes some ten minutes, and while the pilot is checking out the externals, Mark Wetzel straps into his seat and begins to fire-up the cockpit.

'I begin an initial check while the pilot is strapping in, and starting up the engines. As most things are computerized, after plugging in the

DTM and the mission dynamics I do a BITE check and ensure all the bits are working and on line. Once I am happy I "read" the DTM information to ensure that it is what I planned, then I check the altimeter settings and begin to set up the CRTs. Once the desired steering points are loaded from the DTM into the Nav system, the planned course and turn points are displayed as overlays on the moving map. I then preview these points to ensure they are laid on the correct map. With all this done there's not a whole lot more to do. Unlike the F-4, the systems fire up really fast, and without a traditional "check-list" to go through the whole sequence only takes around 5 to 10 minutes and we are ready to roll.'

Such was the case in the early hours of 16 January 1991, when Mark Wetzel, assigned temporarily to the 335th TFS, blasted off into the Saudi night sky for his part in the initial attack on H2 airfield deep in Iraq. Armed with twelve Mk 82 bombs, four AIM-9 Sidewinder missiles, two

wing tanks and the Lantirn pods, Mark Wetzel and pilot Fred Butress head for their target. Once established on their outbound heading, Bones runs a series of systems checks as they speed toward their tanker rendezvous. 'To achieve maximum surprise the tanking was undertaken "Com-Out". Thankfully everything went well and after we gassed up we ducked down to low level just before we crossed the border, setting the TFR to 350ft. As we sped toward the target I began to set up the attack systems.'

Nearing the target the crew are aware from orbiting AWACS that 'bandits' are airborne in their area, CAP'ing at 7–10,000ft with the Eagles running beneath them. 'Right now I am looking at the radar and listening to AWACS and checking the TSD (Tactical Situation Display) and looking at our position on the moving map, ensuring we are on track. Still aware that off to our east the bad guys are still around, but so far posing no threat to our ingress.' As they hit their third waypoint, the

Above: Taxiing past other 'Eagles Eagles', Mark Wetzel and Fred Butress head for the main runway. (Andy Evans)

Right: Pre-flight preparation on the Echo Eagle. (Andy Evans)

High-Tech Attackers

Jordan highway, in their 2 o'clock an AAA battery opens up on them. Keeping a watchful eye on the RHWR Bones continues to monitor and align the systems. At about twenty miles out the aircraft pitches up to a pre-planned medium altitude and, using the radar, Mark Wetzel calls up a 'patch map' of the area. With the radar in 'Map-Mode' Bones moves the marker cursor around the display and marks the spot on his selected target. The quality of the map image is excellent, and one that an earlier generation Wizzo would have given anything to have available; the quality is that of a black-and-white photograph. Once the target is marked Mark Wetzel transfers the image to one of the CRTs and sets up the bombing run.

The target is now locked into the system and the FLIR is updating the attack system as they run in. The lights of H2 grow closer and as the aiming 'pipper' covers the target the aircraft rolls inverted

Left: Full afterburner engaged as the Eagles blast off from Seymour Johnson runway.

Opposite page, bottom: Groundcrew and aircrew prepare the Echo Eagle for flight, and the aircraft's extensive canopy is very evident. (Staff Sergeant Rich Covington)

Below: Layout of the back-seat instrument panel of the F-15 Strike Eagle. (Courtesy of McDonnell Douglas)

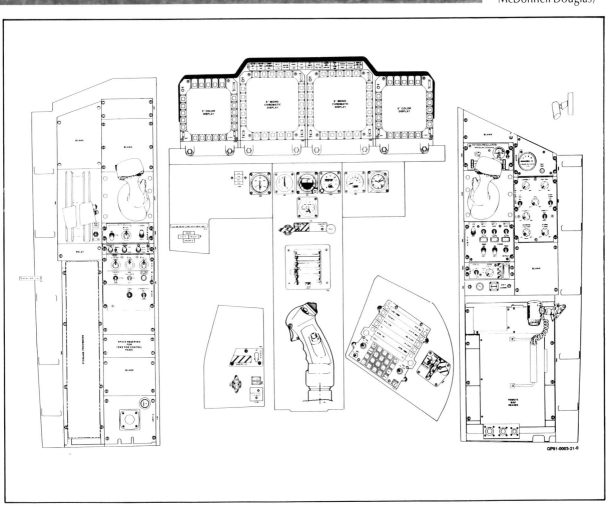

into a wings-level dive. The automatic system cues up the Mk82s and 'pickles' them, indicates all bombs away as the aircraft rolls into a 90-degree left turn and speeds away. Checking over his shoulder, Mark Wetzel sees the bombs hit as they once again engage the TFR for a low-level egress. 'Everything happened so quickly,' he says. 'With all these automated systems in control it ran on rails.' Concentrating now on the RHWR, the big thing now is deconfliction, not hitting other aircraft, and not being bounced by fighters. 'As we continued our egress, we became party to one of the most bizzare events of the whole Gulf

War,' he says. On the nose, 180 degrees out, no kidding, 3,000ft above, coming right at us was a pair of MiG-29s! Obviously on a GCI (Ground Controlled Intercept). I am convinced they didn't know we were there, and they didn't have their radar on as I had no indication on the RHWR. They got to where the ground controller figured we must be and began an instrument turn, with one of them breaking off. Right then our wing man sees an air-to-air missile come off the first MiG. He immediately goes defensive, but seeing the missile isn't guiding on them comes back to course. What happens now is the missile streaks

Below: An F-15E from Luke AFB cruises over the desert. (McDonnell Douglas)

away and scores a direct hit on the other MiG which explodes in a ball of flame, at which the first MiG, obviously distracted, flies straight into the desert! My experience has made me even more convinced of the excellent abilities of this airplane. My own (unbiased) opinion is that two seats is still the way to go, but I consider that in single-seat attack, especially at night, and even using Lantirn, the workload must be impossible, whereas with two crew it's acceptable.'

The F-15E will be the last stand for the Wizzo unless a future-generation aircraft is developed to carry two crew. The current plot in attack aircraft is to rely more and more on automated systems for one-man operations. Much of the advanced technology in the Strike Eagle may well be commonplace in future aircraft, but as far as today goes, Mark Wetzel and the other Echo Wizzos are proving their worth and setting standards that will be hard to match.

Acknowledgements. Thanks to Captain Mark Wetzel, Major Jay Barber, PAO at Seymour Johnson, Staff Sergeant Rich Covington, Staff Sergeant Rick Schick, Major Dave Cannon at RAF Lakenheath, McDonnell Douglas, Mike Kopack.

Electronic Warfare &

THE WORLD OF AERIAL WARFARE is one of constant challenge and development, and in the field of airborne electronics this is very apparent. Electronic Warfare, or EW to give it its common name, saw its real beginnings during the Second World War with the advent of radar, and the means to deceive it using 'countermeasures' such as 'window' and the like. Over the next decades more and more sophisticated aircraft have been developed to further the use of EW. Many of today's combat types carry their own EW equip-ment in the form of Jammer Pods, chaff and flare dispensers to protect themselves in the combat zone. There are, however, a number of specialist EW aircraft that provide stand-off jamming, using extremely powerful emitters, or fly into combat with formations of aircraft to confuse and disable tracking systems. Other specialist aircraft form the other part of the EW chain in defence suppres-sion, using advanced systems to sniff out hostile radar sites that could track and launch Surface to Air Missiles (SAMs), and using Anti-Radar Mis-siles shut them down.

Below: Front end of an EA6 Prowler showing the Gold Tinted canopies to good effect, and the menacing HARM missile on the wing pylon. (Mike Kopack)

Defence Suppression

Most of these specialists are variants of existing combat types, such as the EF-111 Raven which is a development of the F-111, or the F-4G Wild Weasel Phantom, which is an anti-radar development of the classic F-4. Other examples under development are the Tornado ECR and, although it is not a dedicated EW platform, the RAF uses its Tornado GR.1s to carry the specialized BAe ALARM anti-radar missile, which is a fire and forget system.

■ **EA-6B Prowler.** This is an unusual inclusion in this section, because the Prowler has not one but three back-seat flyers! Based on the A-6 Intruder, the EA-6 has an extended forward fuselage, housing a crew of four, consisting of a pilot and three Electronic Countermeasures Officers (ECMOs), and provides the US Navy with an outstanding carrier-based tactical jamming platform. The basis of the success of the Prowler comes from the remarkable AN/ALQ-99 Tactical Jamming System, control of which can be taken by any of the ECMOs in a variety of modes. As can be expected, the EA-6 crews have been

Below: EA-6B Prowler rolls in to tank. (Curtiss Knowles)

Electronic Warfare & Defence Suppression

extensively trained, and the ECMOs have a 26-week intensive course at 'Prowler University' or VAQ-129, following three months at NAS Pensacola.

The intense workload is split between the Prowler's three ECMOs, although their duties are interchangeable. EMCO-1, seated next to the pilot, operates half the TJS, while ECMO-2, seated behind him, operates the other half, therefore ensuring that all frequencies are cov-ered. ECMO-3, seated behind the pilot, operates the ALQ-92 COMJAM system. In the backseats the ECMOs each have a single TV tab at eye level, which in turn is surrounded by instrumentation. Their view outside is limited to across their left- or right-hand sides, although the front seat ECMO has the better view out.

The primary function of the EA-6 is to provide air strikes with jamming protection, although it can be called upon to perform EW support for a

Below: EA-6B Prowler taking on gas. (Curtiss Knowles)

Right: Close up of the EA6 Prowler cockpits. (Andy Evans)

task force, or defence of the fleet. Each type of mission places different demands on the crew. Things can certainly get hectic when the crew are working at full stretch, but the fact remains that for such a small aircraft the ECMOs can cope with an unenviable number of threats, a fact no doubt confirmed by those they have supported.

■ **Tornado ECR.** Just entering service with the Luftwaffe is the Tornado ECR (Electronic Combat and Reconnaissance), the latest variant of the successful multi-national design. Seeking an improved recce capability, and moving away from the traditional wet film process (similar to the Tornado GR.1A) combined with a capability for the Suppression of Enemy Air Defence (SEAD), the ECR Tornado is breaking new ground. Having many advanced features, it provides the back-seater with a new role in interpreting the information from the EW sensors, and obtaining tactical recce. On the wingroots emitter location systems pinpoint hostile ground radar stations, and the back-seater can define the threat and dispatch anti-radar missiles to deal with it. Under the nose, in place of the Mauser cannon, a Forward Looking Infra-Red and an Infra-Red Linescanner are located in a ball fairing. These sensors provide

horizon to horizon coverage which the back-seater views on one of his TV Tabs, allowing him to analyse the sensor data in real time, mark points of interest, freeze frame for close inspection and provide an in-flight report of his findings. The ECR uses video tape for its recce sensors, similar to the method employed by the RAF's GR.1As, and allows much more flexibility than the wet film process.

In the back seat, the navigator has all the traditional Tornado IDS instruments, and within the systems he is able to call up his specialized displays for threat location and recce. The Emmiter Locator System contains a library of hostile emitter data which, coupled with the ability to use IR sensors not only to locate and dispatch hostile radar but also to provide near real-time reconnaissance of the area, makes the ECR Tornado a true force multiplier.

Left: Although not a dedicated EW aircraft, the RAF's Tornados can carry the British Aerospace developed ALARM anti-radar missile, two of which can be seen on the shoulder pylons of this desert coloured GR.1. (BAe)

Below: German Tornado ECR. (Cristoff Kugler)

Below: German
Tornado ECR lights its
burners at take-off.
(Cristoff Kugler)

Left, top and bottom:
EF-111 Ravens. (Andy
Evans)

■ **EF-111 Raven.** Built around a much modified F-111A, the EF-111 owes much of its success to the Navy's EA-6 Prowler, and its exceptional ALQ-99 Tactical Jamming System. The aircraft is operated by a two-man crew, a pilot and an ECMO who operates the jamming systems from the right-hand seat. Similar to the EA-6, the sensitive systems are mounted in an enlarged tail fairing, and while the Prowler carries 'podded' jammers, the EF-111 mounts the rest of its systems internally. In the cockpit the ECMO has control of all the traditional systems of the F-111 such as radar and radios. He has, however, the main responsibility for the TJS, and has a multi-function cockpit display and keyboard to achieve this. The EF-111 has a much upgraded version of the ALQ-99 system, tailored for one-man operation, thus allowing a single EF-111 ECMO to do the work of three EA-6 EMCOs, by virtue of a more automated system!

F-4G Phantom: 'Wild Weasel EWO'

During the Vietnam War, the losses to US aircraft from surface-to-air missiles (SAMs) began to grow at an unacceptable rate. The USAF looked hard at putting into the combat area specialized fast-jet platforms, able to 'sniff out' and destroy SAM sites by homing in on their radar emissions. The first aircraft to be specifically modifed for the role was the F-105 Thunderchief, equipped with Shrike anti-radar missiles and an advanced Radar Homing Warning receiver. Nicknamed 'Wild Weasel', these aircraft carried a new kind of back-seater, the Electronic Warfare Officer, the EWO or 'Bear'.

By the end of the conflict the Thud had been uprated with even more sophisticated equipment, but by then they were a little long in the tooth, and a replacement was necessary. The answer was found in yet another variant of the Phantom. Initially the Wild Weasel mission was carried by modified F-4Cs, and these began operations towards the end of the war. Although some F-4Ds and F-4Es had also been configured to carry out the mission, with externally mounted detection gear, in order to meet the full requirements of the role a totally new version was developed, the F-4G Advanced Wild Weasel, which was a much-modified variant of the F-4E, and better equipped to carry out the hunter-killer role. The F-4G differs from the E in that it has the internal gun replaced by a chin pod housing radar detection sensors, and the addition of a further

Below: F-4Gs. (Curtiss
Knowles)

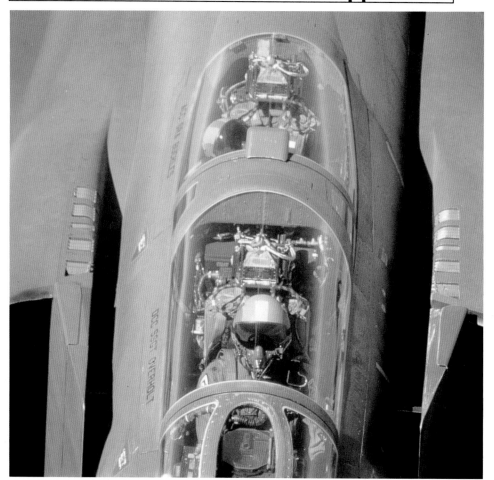

pod on the tail, together with numerous aerials along the spine.

Internally the installation of the highly complex APR-38 Radar detection system gave the Weasels and unparalleled capability to look for hostile radar emissions. Because of the sensitive nature of the EWO's job and systems, it has not been practicable to look in depth at his mission, but in order to get an idea of the EWO's task as a back-seat flyer, the following is a brief look at his 'world'.

At the heart of the F-4G's rear cockpit is the AN/APR-38 RHWR with its Homing and Warning Computer system (HAWC). This sophisticated system allows the EWO to 'see' the threat information presented to him on a display which contains a triangulation, distance and bearing, and supplies data for weapons delivery directly to the ordnance. The HAWC displays the threat information to the EWO in a similar manner to the RHWR in an F-4E, but in the Weasel it is larger and far more comprehensive in its abilities. The

main display in front of the EWO is a large Plan Position Indicator (PPI) situated to the left of his radar scope. This display enables him to maintain overall control of the proceedings. The HAWC receives information from its sensors, and automatically determines priorities to the threat emissions, of which fifteen can be monitored at any one time, depending on how the EWO has set the system: the greatest threat is indicated by the triangle surrounding it. If necessary this can be overridden by the EWO to reflect another target he feels to be more important. He does this by manually placing a diamond symbol over it on the display, and the computer then re-calculates the threat information.

To the right of the PPI are two further TV-style displays which are the 'Homing' and 'Panoramic' indicators, and these allow the EWO to investigate the emitter frequencies in greater detail. Further to aid frequency detection, the EWO is presented with a number of varying tones in his headset, which are linked to the system, and an

experienced EWO is able to recognize any subtle changes in these tones.

Once the F-4G is in a threat area and the system is looking at the emissions, the EWO monitors the threats, and after a target has been selected, either manually by the EWO or automatically by the HAWC, it is fed into the attack system. The aircraft may be flying an attack pattern and the computer remembers the position of the threat on its display and then runs an attack course with the target information being fed directly to the anti-radar missiles such as Shrike, HARM or Standard ARM. Once the weapon has been sequenced by the EWO, providing the radar emissions are within the missile's parameters, it is launched for the kill.

In training, a typical Weasel mission would take about six hours to complete, although the actual flying time might only be one hour. The planning and briefing phase is extensive, and includes detailed routeing and a detailed description of what will be expected of the EWO in each area. New Weasel flyers are usually assigned to the 562nd FS, and these are generally experienced F-4 crews, although with the continuing withdrawal of the Phantom more and more first tourists are being taken. The basic course starts on the F-4E, and only when they know the machine inside out are they allowed near the Wild Weasel. The Ground Phase sees the crews having 310 hours of instruction on the systems. In Phase 1 the EWO or 'Baby Bear' has seven sorties, and in Phase 2 the pilot and EWO fly 22 sorties.

The F-4 played an important part in the Gulf War, flying alongside the Allied attack packages and successfully shutting down any Iraqi radar sites that they encountered. With the only possible replacement – the F-15G – still a while away, the F-4G seems set to soldier on for some time yet, and will have the distinction of being not only the last front-line version of the Phantom still in service, but along with the Strike Eagle it will be the last bastion for the Back-Seat Flyers in the US Air Force.

Opposite page, top: A Spangdahlem-based F-4G taxies out. (Cristoff Kugler)

Opposite page, bottom: A classic shot of a Phantom in flight.

Left: Two good views of the cramped Phantom cockpit, the instruments severely restricting the view forward. (Curtiss Knowles)

Reconnaissance

ANOTHER OF THE BASIC TASKS of warfare is to obtain good battlefield intelligence concerning an enemy's movements and positions. The value of aerial recce was recognized during the First World War with balloons and later with aircraft.

Since that time a number of specialized aircraft have been developed to meet the need. Many have been single-seat aircraft adapted to carry pod-mounted cameras, such as the Jaguar and Mirage F.1C; others have been variants of single-seater aircraft such as the RF-5 Tigereye. There

Below: F-14 Tomcat can be fitted with the TARPS pod on the underfuselage pylons. (US Navy)

are, however, a few two-seater recce aircraft currently in service throughout the world, and one of the latest, the Tornado GR.1A, is dealt with in detail in this chapter.

■ **SR-71 Blackbird.** Perhaps one of the most

recognizable shapes in the sky is the Mach-3 SR-71, an aircraft designed, developed and flown in total secrecy, and used for high-speed, high-altitude clandestine reconnaissance. The aircraft carries a crew of two, a pilot and an RSO (Reconnaissance Systems Officer) who sits in the

back seat under a separate clamshell canopy, behind sheets of heat-resistant glass. Both crew wear astronaut-type 'space-suits', and follow extensive pre-fight procedures similar to space missions! The RSO has command of some of the most unique and comprehensive reconnaissance systems available, able to cover sixty to eighty thousand square miles every hour.

■ **RF-4 Phantom.** Another variant of the successful McDonnell Douglas design is the so-called 'Photo-Phantom', in service with the US Air Force and Marines, and with the air forces of Germany and Israel to name but two. The US military operate the RF-4B for the Marines and RF-4C for the Air Force, these aircraft having a modified nose section to accommodate cameras and other sensors, but no provision for Sparrow missiles. The RF-4 carries an impressive array of intelligence-gathering equipment such as the KA-55 and 56 panoramic cameras (in the USAF versions), and the DS72 and 85 (in the Marines), an APQ-102 Sideways Looking Infra Red (SLIR) and

an AAS-18 Linescan. In the back seat the Wizzo has control of these sensors, and is able to 'mark' areas of interest by putting an arrow on the film, as well as having a degree of control as to the quality of the image. Flying the back seat of the RF-4 is a specialized task; the WSO is able to use the systems to compensate for cloud cover, day or night operations, and sensor sensitivity, as well as SLIR range. He has a cramped work-station common to the Phantom, with the extra 'recce-bits' taking up more space, such as the camera selection panel which contains not only camera operations but the switches for the other sensors and a film-remaining counter and a device recording the number of 'flash' cartridges available.

■ **F-14 Tomcat 'Tarps'.** With the retirement of the RA-5C Vigilante and the RF-8 Crusader, the US Navy found itself without any credible recce assets. The answer was found in the Tactical Aerial Reconnaissance Pod System (Tarps). Designed as an interim system until a dedicated

Above: The futurustic shape of the SR-71 Blackbird silhouetted against the blue sky. (Curtiss Knowles)

Top right: German RF-4E. (Andy Evans)

Right: RF-4C taking on gas, good view of the cramped rear crew station. (Curtiss Knowles)

recce aircraft was introduced into service, it was originally earmarked to be carried by the A7-E Corsair. However it was tested on an F-14 with great success, and the higher speed of the Tomcat proved no problem for the Tarps system. A number of Tomcats were converted to carry Tarps, which is mounted on an under-fuselage station, five in place of one of the Phoenix missiles. The controls for the Tarps pod are mounted in the rear cockpit with the sensors being operated by the RIO, provision for the extra switches being made on his left-hand console. Some 34 Tomcats are able to carry Tarp, the normal complement being two per Squadron.

Tornado GR.1A: Recce Navigator

'One of the most important parts of the Tornado GR.1A is its ability to present its recce information in "real-time", and for me as a back-seater it has been an exciting challenge to be part of this new system. Using videotaped information rather than the traditional "wet film" process, I can actually look at the images as the aircraft flies over a target and even relay vital information in flight. Add to that the Tornado's established low-

level and bad weather capabilities and we have an impressive all-round recce platform.' Comment from Flight Lieutenant Mike 'Tommo' Tomlinson, a Recce Nav serving with No II (AC) Squadron at RAF Laarbruch in Germany, the first RAF unit to be equipped with the BAe-developed Reconnaissance Tornado, another variant of the successful Panavia design.

'Before the arrival of Tornado, the tactical recce role was undertaken in the main by the Jaguar, with a specialist add-on under-fuselage pod which used traditional cameras and methods to gather information. The Jags had no TFR (Terrain Following Radar) or GMR (Ground Mapping Radar), a very limited night capability that relied on IR sensors in the recce pod, and being single-seat, the pilot had not only to fly the aircraft, but also navigate accurately and monitor all the on-board systems. With the two-crew concept in Tornado, the pilot can concentrate on flying the aircraft and avoid hitting the ground, while the back-seater can concentrate on running the systems. The images we get from the systems are excellent and can be enhanced or blown up as necessary. To achieve this quality the aircraft is fitted with two SLIRs and an IRLS (Infra-Red Linescan) giving a sideways and vertical coverage

Above: RF-4C from IDAHO ANG. (Curtiss Knowles)

Right: Taking in the instruments and looking over the pilot's head, this view gives a good indication of the Nav's forward vision. (Andy Evans)

of a target. So if we wanted to look at a radio mast we would stand off to one side and use the SLIR, or if we were looking at a column of vehicles we might go over the top and use the IRLS, so in effect we have horizon-to-horizon coverage. The aircraft has an impressive night capability too, thanks to the TFR and GMR and the use of NVGs for pilot and Nav. With a reliable Nav system it is possible theoretically after take-off to fly automatically on a pre-planned "track", record the appropriate details, and return to base completely "hands-off".'

Mike Tomlinson, aged 32, hails from Castleford in West Yorkshire, and is currently nearing the end of his tour with the Squadron. Influenced by his father's wishes for him to 'learn a trade', he joined the RAF as an engineering apprentice, going through RAF Cosford before being posted to RAF Marham where he worked on the Vulcan. During his apprenticeship he won the Philip Sassoon flying award, and gained his Private Pilot's Licence. This gave him the 'bug' to become an airman rather than groundcrew. His first choice was to be a pilot, but because his eyesight was not of the required standard, he was given the option to train as a navigator. He began his officer training an RAF Cranwell in May 1985,

and on gaining his commission was posted to RAF Finningley for Navigator Training the following November, graduating in March 1987.

'One of the first lessons I learned at Finningley was how to be sick,' he says. 'Finningley is the RAF's Navigation school, and there I learned all the basics of the job, starting with ground school, then into a Dominie for basic radar and route work, then a phase in a two man Jet Provost for a little fast experience, more route work and some DR (dead reckoning) nav training. After a course assessment I was streamed fast-jet Group 1, which is what I wanted, and from there I went to the Low Level Training Squadron (LLTS or LOUTS as the coloquial expression has it) for more work in the back of a Dominie and another phase in a JP, this time doing more work towards running intercepts, and having a very demanding low-level phase desinged to stretch you. Further course assessment led to my future aircraft being

decided as Tornado, and I was to join the Mud Movers in the Ground Attack role. With this route established I was given a further five trips in the JP to familiarize me with the demands of the Tornado world.

'The next step was a posting to a Tactical Weapons unit at RAF Brawdy in Wales to get some 'Fast-Jet' experience in the agile BAe Hawk T.1. Again I learned how to be sick, only this time at a faster speed!' Nothing, however, could have equipped him for flying in the Tornado. 'It was very different to anything I had experienced in training,' he says. 'During the whole syllabus I learned the basics of airmanship, getting used to the back-seat environment and the ethos of SA (Situational Awareness), using the radios, charts, maps, routes and organizing my priorities in the air, dealing with emergencies and scanning my instruments. Eighty per cent of the Nav's time is supposed to be spent looking-out, which at first is

Above: Tornado GR.1 rear cockpit, dominated by the circular CRMPD flanked either side by the two TV tabs. Note the difference from the F4 Phantom, and even the Strike Eagle! (BAe)

Above: SLIR Imagery of a bridge as Mike Tomlinson and Rick Haley speed past. (RAF)

pretty difficult to achieve with so many other things to think about! Gradually the awareness comes as you get used to operating in the back seat.' Having completed the Hawk phase, Mike Tomlinson was sent to the Trinational Tornado Training Establishment at RAF Cottesmore to learn the basics of flying in a Tornado and how to use its systems. On completion of the course he was assigned to the Tornado Weapons Conversion Unit at RAF Honington to learn how to operate the aircraft in front-line service.

After his time with the TWCU he was posted to his first front-line unit, No 31 Squadron at RAF Bruggen, and was soon declared 'combat ready' in the strike attack role. After thirteen months with No 31 Squadron and with the arrival of the Tornado GR.1A into service came a change of direction. 'No II Squadron had just formed and had a requirement for four Navs who were not just out of training and had a minimum of one

year's experience on Tornado. I was one of those chosen, and although at first a little unsure about the posting, I was pleased to be selected for the challenge of bringing this system into front-line service. There was now a different emphasis on the flying, and I had to take more notice of the terrain and the ground, develop the ability to spot equipment and facilities on the ground that could be of importance to friendly forces, and learn how to get the best out of the new recce system, and iron out the bugs.

'On the ground the difference was also apparent from the strike side. We had slide training, looking at a large amount of shots of potential enemy equipment as well as friendly, developing our abilities instantly to recognize things as we encountered them. Then there were the PIs, the Photographic Interpreters, vital to the success of the mission, as they were tasked with exploiting the tapes we brought back in their specialized interpretation centre, and learning to work with them in order to achieve the desired result.'

The Tornado is the product of multi-national co-operation between Britain, Germany and Italy, and the Tornado GR.1A has been specifically modified for the recce role, although it retains all the bombing capabilities of the strike version. The aircraft assigned to No II Squadron are modified early-production GR.1s, although the unit's sister Squadron, No 13, have received new-build aircraft. The modifications are most noticeable on the forward fuselage with the deletion of the twin Mauser cannon and the addition of two 'windows' either side of the fuselage for the SLIR, and a 'tear-drop' fairing under the fuselage which houses the IRLS. Inside the aircraft are located six video recorders, three prime and three secondary. Using the three secondary units the Nav can review recorded images in flight, and compile an edited version of the key features, while the three primary VCRs continue recording.

The rear cockpit of the Tornado is much larger than that any of contemporary RAF aircraft. That said, however, the view outside is restricted because of the bulkhead behind the Nav and the large intakes on each side of the aircraft, just below the canopy. Centred around radar and navigation systems, the first thing you notice are the two TV tabulator displays and the circular radar/moving-map display, the CRMPD, with their associated soft key function pads.

'It takes a little getting used to the keypad, and the keys change in their notation depending upon which "page" is being displayed on the tab,' says Tommo. The rear left-hand side of the cockpit contains the air filter for the AR5 system, and also contains the switches for the lighting and the Secondary Attitude Reference System, the SARS, which forms part of the Inertial Navigation System, the INS. Also situated in this section is the cockpit voice recorder, which is also used to load the route information into the main computer via a cassette tape formatted on the GCPU.

In front of the Nav and to his right-hand side are the chaff/flare controls and the RHWR, and along the bottom line of the centre console are the Nav-Mode selector, steering selector and height sensor selector. Directly above these is the CRMPD and above that an altimeter, air speed indicator and angle-of-attack indicator. Below these and to the left are an artificial horizon and weapons control panel No 1, the pilot having panel No 2 in front of

Below: Rick Haley checks around the aircraft in the HAS while 'Tommo' climbs into the back seat. (Mike Tomlinson)

Right: A ground technician loads the video tapes into the aircraft's VCRs. (Andy Evans)

Below right: Take-off as seen from the Nav's position. (Andy Evans)

his stick, the Nav having main control of weapons selection.

The two TV Tabs are the link between man and main computer, and these have three basic formats. The 'plan' format displays the overall mission plan, with the various waypoints being shown as letters, 'A', 'B', 'C', etc. Fixed points are indicated by a number, '1', '2', '3', etc., and targets by the letters 'X', 'Y', 'Z'. The aircraft's current position is displayed as a small circle which is overlaid with a lat/long grid. The 'Nav' format shows the aircraft's position at centre screen, surrounded by a circle through which is placed a vertical line representing the current track. Information such as the next waypoint can also be seen on this display. The third format is 'fix/attack', and this represents a 'bird's-eye' view of the aircraft's position relative to the planned target, which enables the Nav to compare his radar picture with this simplified image, allowing him better to assess the situation at a glance. The Recce Tornado has a fourth format, 'Recce' format, which displays the sensor's view on his left-hand TV tab.

At front left is the recce control panel, unique to the GR.1A, and this generates a number of 'windows' on the TV tab, controls the VCRs and

allows the replay of images on the screen for the Nav to interrogate further. In front of the Nav, between his legs, is his hand controller, which interphases with the CRMPD to mark fixes and control the system marker.

Operationally the recce mission appears to be of a complex nature, given the sheer volume of sensors and systems fitted to the Tornado GR.1A. We follow Mike Tomlinson on a typical training sortie in Germany. 'We always like to be tasked with a target and our detailed planning begins from there. The sortie starts in the planning room inside the ARF. A normal training trip takes in five targets, and on this trip one will be a bridge which is of "importance" to friendly forces, and we will be flying as a singleton.' The pilot for the trip is Flight Lieutenant Rick Haley, a veteran of the Gulf War, credited with having flown the longest recce mission. The pilot and Nav pilot plot the location of the targets on a 1:50,000 Ordnance Survey map. Consideration is given to the lighting conditions (the sun's position can be important in daytime ops, and can aid in visually acquiring the target). Mike Tomlinson checks the NOTAMS, and the avoidance of towns and restricted areas on the route are noted. After taking into account the weather and endurance, the route is drawn on

to a standard half-mil (1:500,000) OS map.

Once the route has been determined 'Tommo' takes it to the CPGS and places it on the systems magnetic table. By feeding in the location of Laarbruch, the aircraft's HAS position plus any other reference features, the electronic sensor system of the CPGS will automatically record the lat/long of each target. Furthermore, by 'walking' the electronic cursor around the route, Mike Tomlinson inserts the position of the appropriate targets. This information is downloaded on to a cassette tape which is subsequently loaded into the aircraft's computer. The Nav can also mark points of interest with an asterisk, around which the computer marks and places a 'one-mile' circle, and this enables the recce kit to switch on when the aircraft reaches that point.

'Good planning is essential,' says Tommo. 'We have to look carefully at our position relative to the target to obtain the best view. The bridge, we plan to fly offset at about one hundred yards, to get the required image. An offset position is always desirable as it allows us visually to examine the target as a back up if by some chance the recce kit should fail. Because this is a single-ship sortie, the brief is a continuation of the planning stage, as we have both been involved

Left: Across the wing shot of take-off. (Andy Evans)

Below left: Speeding down the runway. (Mike Tomlinson)

Below: Once airborne the crew fly in TFR to their first target. (Andy Evans)

with the specifics. Rick, however, may discuss the way he intends to look at the target and what he is looking to achieve from the sortie. Our targets are categorized, and there are seventeen categories from which to select. These range from airfields, factories and the like.'

Rick Haley reinforces the mission objective and after outbrief the crew collect their G-pants, life-jackets, gloves and helmets and walk to the jet. Once inside the HAS the aircraft will already have the power on and the ground crew will have set the INS to align with the HAS co-ordinates, and while Rick Haley does the walk round, Mike Tomlinson climbs into the back seat and sets about firing up the systems and bringing the recce sensors on line. As Rick Haley straps in Mike Tomlinson inputs the CPGS cassette into the main computer, and does a map follow to check the relevent details such as targets and turning-points have gone in. Once satisfied, he continues to switch on the SARS, the Doppler, Laser, and checks the fuel, electrics and hydraulics.

'The start-up sequence is very quick for such a complex jet,' says Tommo, 'and very little is said between pilot and Nav, except to confirm readiness and check comparative gauge readings in both cockpits. The only "delay" is caused by the Stores Management System as it does its BITE tests. It is essential that the SMS is working correctly so that the externally mounted fuel and ECM pods can be quickly jettisoned in the case of an emergency.' Once satisfied that all the systems are functioning, the crew are ready to roll. 'Having ensured full and free movement in the controls, the pilot flashes the nosewheel landing light and we are marshalled out of the HAS. On the way to the runway we run through the pre-take-off checks:

Navigator	Pilot
'Wing sweep.'	'25 degrees.'
'Airbrakes.'	'In and locked.'
'Flaps.'	'Mid.'
'Trims.'	'Set for take-off.'
'Cross drive clutch.'	'Auto light out.'
'Selective emergency	
jettison.'	'Selected.'
'Flight Controls.'	'Full and free
	movement.'
'Hydraulics.'	'Left on, right auto,
	correct pressure in
	both.'
'Emergency power	
system.'	'Auto position.'

Below: In its element! Having excellent low-level abilities, the Tornado GR.1A speeds at low level across the sea. (Andy Evans)

Right: A classic study of the GR.1A. (Andy Evans)

'Fuel.'	'Check contents both cockpits, normal selected, check fin is feeding.'
'Ignition.'	'Normal selected.'
'Oxygen.'	'Check breathing, contents flow.'
'Intake anti-icing.'	'Auto.'
'External lights.'	'All functioning.'
'Command eject system.'	'Both seats locked.'
'Canopy.'	'Closed and locked, caption light out.'
'Safety pins.'	'Removed and stowed.'
'Take-off emergency brief.'	'Abort for AC/DC red caption, burner blow out or engine failure. Select thrust reverse override. If airborne, both engines in combat power, ensure landing gear is retracting. If

handling becomes difficult, call Nav to jettison external stores. If it is still impracticable to stay with the aircraft, call 'Eject, Eject' and the Nav will take both crew out.'

Mike Tomlinson talks to the tower to confirm that they are taxiing and obtains wind speed and the pressure settings, and the runway to be used. At the end of the runway the crew perform their final checks. Rick Haley checks that the thrust reverser indicators are out and that normal nosewheel steering is selected. The engines are run up against the brakes, then up to max dry power. A check that the 'burners are functioning and the brakes are released. As they roll down the runway Mike Tomlinson checks the speed and ensures that both cockpit readouts agree. At 155kts Rick Haley pulls back the stick and they are airborne. The gear comes up at 225kts and the flaps are retracted and the 'burners de-selected at 250kts, with the master arm switch being set to standby.

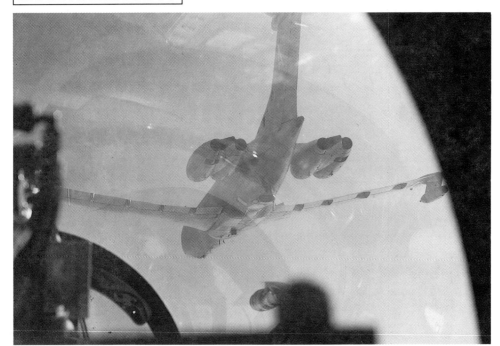

Left: Two shots of a back-seater's view, picking up a VC-10 tanker. (Andy Evans)

At 350kts the wings are swept back to 45 degrees. During this time Mike Tomlinson has been talking to the tower, advising them of the aircraft's departure. Rick Haley selects the TFR and as they speed away to their first waypoint Mike Tomlinson is continually checking his systems for performance and accuracy.

No II Squadron always fly to their first planned target using the TFR, simulating IFC (Instrument Flying Conditions), so that the pilot can check that all is working as it should. 'For me as a Nav,' says Mike Tomlinson, 'my time is divided between a number of tasks, most important being keeping a sharp look-out. My area of responsi-

Right: Speeding at low level towards their target. (Andy Evans)

Right: The navigator's rearward view of a second Tornado closing in. (Andy Evans)

bility is the 3-9 line and 85 per cent of the back-seater's work should be "outside" the cockpit. I am also responsible for the operation of the Skyshadow ECM pod and the Boz-107 chaff/flare dispenser, and the constant monitoring of the RHWR, the fuel state, the condition of the Nav-kit as well as advising the pilot of turn directions, target data, speed changes, terrain information and possible threats. With an operational height of 100ft, maintaining that altitude in a two-man jet like Tornado is quite easy, provided that the Nav has full confidence in his pilot. I think that it takes longer for the Nav to get used to flying at this level than it does for a pilot, and he needs to

Above: Tornado GR.1A. (Andy Evans)

Right: Plan view as the crew pitch up to medium altitude for their next way point.

build up trust with the guy up front.'

After locating the first target successfully, Rick Haley now flies 'hands-on' to the next. 'The next target is a bridge, and we step down to a lower altitude on our run, in order to get a better look and allow the sensors the best chance of a good image. Although the recce system can be pre-programmed to start at a set point, for this particular target, as the aircraft approaches its next IP, Mike Tomlinson switches on the recce kit and begins to ready himself to report on the target. Accelerating now to 480kts, Mike confirms that all the systems are functioning, and Rick Haley confirms. The aircraft will fly off-set to the bridge and use the SLIR to record the image as they fly past, using the IRLS to look inside the spans.

'We can afford to bank the aircraft up to 30 degrees in toward the target', says 'Tommo', 'so that the Navy, who can't see through the pilot, gets about a ten-second look at the bridge as it passes down the side.' 'On track,' calls Tommo . . . 'Kits running . . . good mark . . . speed OK.' In the distance Rick Haley sees the target and begins to describe what he sees as the aircraft

approaches. 'Confirm taking down the left-hand side,' announces Haley. 'Banking . . . now.' As soon as 'Tommo' sees the bank come on it is heads out. The general rule of thumb is that the pilot describes the top sections and the Nav looks at what is below. 'Tommo' hits the 'freeze' button on the recce display as they go past, so that they have a picture of the target to refer to as they come off the target. 'Beam and deck,' says Tommo, 'Four spans . . . steel construction . . . Concrete Base.' Mike Tomlinson notes its composition, any defences or activity around it, and any alternate crossings within 200 metres over the river. As fast as their approach . . . the bridge is gone – captured on tape, and noted both written and verbally, and like a black dart the Tornado speeds to its next point.

A quick check of the systems, and Mike Tomlinson continues to note his observations. It may be that he will be required to transmit a

Reconnaissance

report as an If-Rep (In Flight-Report), in which case he has a set reporting format to which he must ahdere. 'Bravo . . . Target number.' 'Charlie . . . Beam and Deck.' 'Charlie 2 Concrete . . . 5 span . . . 2 lane.' 'Delta . . . No defences seen.', and so on.

It is important that the Nav accurately record his Vis-Rep (Visual-Report) because when he gets back to base he will have to build a picture for the photographic interpreters, who assume that the video has not worked until they see the imagery. When they compare his report with the pictures the result will be posted in the ARF next day for all to see (and comment on). Anything of interest can be reviewed by the Nav as they continue to the next target, and anything of interest can be marked on the tape for later exploitation by the PIs.

Pushing on, the crew capture the final three targets on tape with no hitches and head back to Laarbruch. 'With all the recce information now on the tapes, as we head back I press the "edit" button, and the system sorts through all the points on the tape that I have "marked" as being of interest, and this allows for quick analysis when we get down. During this phase I am heads in looking at the tape on the left-hand monitor.' Coming back to Laarbruch the crew go through their pre-recovery checks:

120

Left: A German
Tornado. (Stuart Black)

Navigator	Pilot
'Wingsweep 25.'	Check.'
'Airbrakes are in.'	'Check.'
'SPILS.'	'Off.'
'Fuel is 161.'	'Check.'
'Flaps down.'	
'Gear down.'	
'Hook light is out.'	
'Harnesses both tight and	'Check.'
locked.'	
'Brakes.'	'Brakes good.'
'Nosewheel steering,	
low light is on.'	'Check.'
'Three greens in the back.'	'Three greens.'

Other checks include setting the radio-altimeter to zero, and switching off the RHWR to prevent any distracting alarms during the landing. Mike Tomlinson advises the tower of their return as they reach a point twenty miles from the runway.

Below left: GR.1A rolls
out of its HAS. (Mike
Tomlinson)

Below: GR.1As break
to land. (Andy Evans)

As they roll in at 400kts at 1,000ft, the tower advises of current weather, which will dictate either a radar or a visual approach. At three miles Rick Haley calls 'initials', and after acknowledgement they pitch into the break. Calling 'finals', full flap is selected to peg the speed as 190kts and Mike Tomlinson calculates the touchdown speed at 160kts. Having lost 200kts in the break, a further 30kts are lost in the final turn.

Watching the Precision Approach Path Indicator Lights, Rick Haley touches down just on the 'piano keys' at the end of the runway. Mike Tomlinson checks that the wing lift dump spoilers are deployed as the nosewheel is slowly lowered and the thrust reversers (the 'buckets') are activated to slow the speed. At 50kts the reversers are set to idle to stop hot gases being ingested into the engines, and having already contacted the Squadrons Ops Centre while airborne, Rick calls in again to let them know they are down and their current serviceability state. If they have not been required to give an airborne If-Rep, they can do this on the way back to the HAS.

At the HAS, a member of the PI team is waiting for them and while the engines are still running the tapes are unloaded from the forward fuselage and speedily dispatched to the waiting PIs, who have a mere 45 minutes to deliver their initial Ex-Rep on the main points of the mission. After shutdown Rick Haley and Mike Tomlinson go to the ARF and then into the RIC (Reconnaissance Interpretation Centre) for what is really the most important part of the mission. 'We discuss our Vis-Reps with the PIs,' says Tommo, 'and depending on the complexity of the sortie, this could take a further 45 to 50 minutes. We also write out our reports and pass them to the PIs who then take our notes, imagery and voice recordings

Reconnaissance

Right: Tanking from a VC-10. (Andy Evans)

Below: Mike Tomlinson's previous unit, No 31 Squadron, formates for the camera. (Andy Evans)

Opposite page: A good view of the Tornado cockpit with the canopy raised as the crew get a final check over before taxi. (Mike Tomlinson)

and do a more detailed report after the initial Ex-Rep is completed. Obviously it is vitally important to arm the PIs with as much information as we can, so our verbal comments and written notes all add to the overall recce package.

'We hold true the saying "Alone, Unarmed and Unafraid", as the Tornado acquitted itself well in the Gulf War, often flying low-level sorties into Iraq unaccompanied, and bringing back vital battlefield information that no doubt contributed to the swift conclusion of the conflict. The Americans were very impressed with our imagery, in fact the 101st Airborne Division asked us to recce a specific area, and we are told that as a result they sat and watched our tape with their maps in one hand, detailing what they saw, and going back to their helicopters armed with good real-time recce, so when their push forward came they had a pretty good idea of what to expect. Such is the excellent ability of the GR.1A, and I am proud to be associated with, not only the aircraft, but one of the oldest Squadrons in the Royal Air Force, who have a fine tradition, and one that the Tornado and the guys that fly them uphold.'

Acknowledgements. My thanks to Mike Tomlinson, Rick Haley, of No II (AC) Squadron, to Mr Michael Hill, CPRO Strike Command, and Wing Commander Colin Tavener, CPRO RAF Germany.

Backseat Changes

THE REAR COCKPIT of the military jet aircraft has seen nearly as many advancements as the airframe itself – from the open cockpit of the early two-seat biplanes to the TV Tabulated air-conditioned command centres of the nineties. Technology has given the back-seater a new role and a new edge; from being merely an 'observer' he is now a 'Weapons Systems Officer' playing a vital role as an integrated member of a combat team.

For the RAF's fast-jet Navigators, the advent of the Tornado, the latest generation of two-man aircraft, has given a new impetus to the role of the back-seater. Perhaps uniquely qualified to comment on the changing role of the back seat is Squadron Leader Bob Fisher, currently serving with No 13 Squadron, who has had more than 30 years' experience in the back seat of the RAF's fast jets, as well as an early tour with the Royal Navy.

'I suppose I was fortunate with my career path,' he says. 'I came straight out of Nav School at Finningley and was given the opportunity to go to Lossiemouth to fly with the Navy when a place became available. I began to fly the Sea Venom to prepare me for life aboard with the Sea Vixen. During this time I was taught low-level Nav, something at that time that wasn't on the course at Finningley. My first impression of the Sea Venom was that of being grateful for a view outside rather than the back end of a Dominie! It was basic to say the least, with side-by-side seating and very rudimentary instruments, but it did enough to get me into the Navy way and prepare me for the Vixen, when once again it was into the dark in the so-called "Coal-Hole".'

'Being in that position was surprisingly enough a great benefit, especially when using the radar, which in those days was not blessed with a daylight viewing screen. Apart from the scope, the other instruments consisted of a Tacan, an Air Position Indicator, a radio, a few basic instruments and a stopwatch. In the Sea Vixen most of what I had learned about Nav stopped, and I was mainly doing intercept work, looking at CAP around the ship, and making accurate times back. The radar itself was interesting as it only had a

short pick-up, a range of some twenty miles, and was reliant upon observer interpretation and my ability to obtain a good 'air-picture' from it, and decide how to action what I saw. There was little else to look at except the radar, but I could see the pilot's flight instruments through his legs, very useful during the fifty or so "cat-shots" I did.'

Moving back to the RAF at the end of his posting, Bob Fisher went to Phantoms, again in

Below: Squadron Leader Bob Fisher. (Andy Evans)

Above: Sea Vixen, similar to the one flown by Bob Fisher early in his career. (Andy Evans)

Right: The front end of a No 13 Squadron Tornado on the Honington tarmac. (Andy Evans)

the air-defence role. In the Phantom he found that technology had advanced with a much more powerful radar, a faster, heavier aircraft and, most importantly for him, a good workplace, with a reasonably good view out from a glazed cockpit. A further posting took him to ground attack, again on the Phantom, putting into practice another set of rules. 'With "Mud-Moving" I spent hours drawing up maps, whereas with Air Defence I drew one map at the beginning of a tour and that lasted the duration!' A further tour took him again to Air Defence with the Phantom, which, '. . . was fascinating, taking to Quick-reaction Alert (QRA) and chasing Russians,' he says. 'Coming up to date, perhaps my greatest challenge was converting to Tornado, and I was one of the first Navs on No 9 Squadron when we came to Honington back in the eighties. Perhaps, a veritable command centre, and presents its information in a way that is precise and understandable, rather than the need to make sense of a lot of 'blips' on a screen. Having said that, though, even with the changes I have seen, I still hold dear to the skills I learned thirty years ago. It is interesting to me that in the Sea Vixen we used regularly to fly at 45,000ft, and as I have gone from aircraft to aircraft, the operating ceiling has got lower and lower, so now we have an operating "floor" of 100ft with Tornado! The role of the fast-jet navigator has changed and become more specialized in nature. In the Phantom there was a lot of interpretation needed, you were working to keep the Nav-Kit updated and trying to keep a look-out. Now, in Tornado, the Nav-Kit actually does the navigating, and we are now almost at the stage where the systems are giving the back-seater the time he needs to keep a look-out and concentrate on the demands of the mission, rather than the demands of the systems.'

Towards the future . . .

The ending of the Cold War and the re-assessment of future defence needs has had a marked effect on many air arms, and both the RAF and USAF have responded with cutbacks and re-structuring of their assets. For the RAF the changes for the back-seater have been two-fold. Right back at basics, the method of navigator training at RAF Finningley has been streamlined to take on board the single aircraft concept in the fast-jet area, the Tornado ADV and IDS, which now bear the brunt of two-seater operations. The Equal Opportunities policy adopted by the RAF has meant that for the first time we can expect female Navs, perhaps in the not too distant future.

The drawdown of forces in Germany, and the disbandment of a number of Tornado squadrons has led to a surplus of navigators. One of the options available was to put these crew into training for helicopter duties, operating in their trained field in the left-hand seat of Chinook, Puma and Wessex aircraft, instead of the usual second pilot. To that end the RAF's helicopter training unit at RAF Shawbury is formulating a new training syllabus to convert a number of the ex-fast jet Navs to the rotary world. At the time of writing the first course is under way, and we await the end product. If successful it could lead to a new way of thinking for the rotary wing aspect of the RAF's operations.

Above: Tornados sit on the Honington ASP ready for their crews; a huge leap forward in technology for the RAF. (Andy Evans)

though, I was even more pleased to be posted to the recce Tornado, and to No 13 Squadron.'

'Sitting in the comparatively spacious backseat, and taking on board its computerized systems and TV tab displays, moving-map that can be overlaid with radar, and a real time recce system, it makes me realize how far we have come in a short space of time. The Tornado's back seat is by comparison to, say, the Sea Vixen,

Backseat Changes

Below: A No 13 Squadron recce Tornado in flight. (Tim Laming)